MW00699274

As a personal survivor of s[...]
this book moves mountains t[...]
helps the reader to understand their feelings and emotions. It is a non-pressuring way to help the survivor realize their self-worth and to find the tools to remain in a life free from abuse and torture. A must read for anyone recovering from the life of sex work or abusive relationships. This book should be distributed to battered women shelters and homes for women who have been trafficked. It will make a huge difference! It is empowering and helpful.

Anonymous, Survivor

As a survivor of sex trafficking and labor trafficking, this is one of the few books that I have read that I could relate to and grow from. This book will give you hope that you are worthy of being loved and that there is hope even in the darkest issues in society. This book will educate you in ways you never thought you could be educated.

Human Trafficking is a hard, societal epidemic that many people struggle to personalize and struggle to understand the truths and horrors that happen to victims. Because of this, many people struggle to balance the truth and tend to either minimize the depths of human trafficking or dramatize the truths. *Leaving the Life* helps us be grounded in the truths of human trafficking by not just sharing real stories from those who have been trafficked but by allowing us to process what we read.

Anonymous, Survivor

Leaving the Life is an approachable tool for freedom. This text incorporates engaging narrative and dialogue with simple, practical reflections. The reader is gently drawn into the story of Elisa in chapters that are easy to digest but not water-down on meaty content. Guiding the reader through non-triggering moments of contemplation ushers in the opportunity for honest reflection, the opportunity for change, and the opportunity for freedom.

Alexis Miller, Not Abandoned International Director and Survivor of Trafficking

I really, really like the book. There aren't a lot of books like this. I like the structure, the story, the variety of lists, the helpful information, and the survivor sharing. I like the telling of Elisa's story because it helps you realize you're not alone.

JH, Survivor

Leaving the Life is a personal and brutally honest snapshot into the realities of transitioning from loving to leaving the Life. Not only does this book offer a relatable story for survivors, it gives helpful reflections and practical steps to help victims of the sex trade and/or sex trafficking exit their current situation and start a new, hope-filled chapter in life. An excellent and helpful read!

Hanna Wade, Sex Trafficking Survivor Advocate and Social Worker

Leaving the Life is raw and real. Elisa's story underscores how victims are vulnerable to manipulation and exploitation. At the same time, it helps them realize their value, their worth, and the fact that they possess the strength and abilities needed to choose a different future.

Sue Ann Heutink, advocate, founder and director of Hope4Justice

This book is a powerful picture of hope - but not the cheap, trivial hope that skips past the pain on a promise of some distant healing or bright future. Instead, the authors invite us into real, nuanced hope that dives into the pain, the fear, the manipulation, and the trauma... and emerges triumphant. Jessa Crisp and Dr. Johnson and are uniquely qualified to write a book like this.

Jeremy Vallerand, CEO, Rescue:Freedom International

An incredibly powerful story of reality for someone "In the Life" finding hope. Contains thought provoking and a helpful guide to exiting the life of grooming and commercial sex trafficking. This book will support courageous survivors to begin their transition into a new life of finding hope and freedom. It will also equip professionals and caregivers to be able to support women on their brave journey to new-found freedom.

Sue Carter, Former Executive Director of Safe from Slavery, anti-trafficking restoration

Dr. Becca and Jessa have written a brutally honest, yet tender scenario everyone caught in the despair of "no hope" will be able to relate to. HOPE breathes through these pages! Open them and discover practical hope and answers for YOU!

Linda Dillow, Speaker and Author of Calm My Anxious Heart

LEAVING THE LIFE

Embracing Freedom from Exploitation

Jessa Dillow Crisp

By
Dr. Becca C. Johnson
Jessa Dillow Crisp
with Karalyn C. Johnson

Published by BridgeHope

P.O. Box 1214, Littleton, CO 80160

info@bridgehopenow.org
www.BridgeHopeNow.org

ISBN: 9780998980041

Keywords: prostitution, exploitation, sex trafficking, commercial sexual exploitation, recovery, restoration, abuse, trauma, intimate partner violence, domestic violence, sex trade, pimp trafficking, familial trafficking

Any Internet addresses (websites, blogs, etc.) and telephone numbers in this book are offered as a resource. They are not intended in any way to be or to imply an endorsement by the authors or publishing organizations, nor do the authors or publishing organizations vouch for the content of these sites and information for the life of this book.

The information contained herein is not intended to be psychotherapy or to substitute for consultation with a licensed health or mental health professional. Application of the contents is at the reader's sole discretion.

Table of Contents

Foreward

I remember the first time I heard someone talk about exploitation and human trafficking. It was after watching a documentary that focused on the differences in human trafficking based on the community and culture in which you live. It highlighted four different locations, one of which was Las Vegas. It was then I realized, "OMG, that's what I went through!" It suddenly hit me; I was a victim of human trafficking! For years, I thought I had been forced into prostitution by my "boyfriend" but reserved "trafficking" for kidnapped kids overseas.

Before that, I didn't know what trafficking truly was or how to put any context to the legal definitions. All I could think of was, "You mean, I wasn't just abused? I didn't just experience domestic violence?" During my time in exploitation, I had even reached out for help from domestic violence shelters. But at that moment, I realized that everything I had been through could actually be summed up in two simple yet complex words: human trafficking. It gave me some closure and a place to start. I finally had words to explain the gravity of what I had experienced.

It was hard to face. I was unknowingly and intentionally pursued by a trafficker. It was all part of his plan, to target me because of my vulnerabilities. Yet it was also a relief to know that there was a name for what I'd gone through and that I wasn't the only one. When I finally got out and started my healing journey, I wondered if I could ever have a life like everyone else I saw around me. I know I am not alone in asking, *Will I ever be normal?*

Later, as I learned about the Stages of Change model, I began to realize that my journey was actually very similar to others. I could see how these stages played out in my lived experience too. At the beginning of my exploitation, I thought, "This is my life. I love him. Our situation is different. Why leave?" But as the threats and violence increased, I began to contemplate the possibility of leaving; I just didn't think it was possible. It took me several years before I realized that I needed to get out.

And even during that confusion and turmoil, I would run and live in a safe home and then go back to him – back and forth, back and forth in a vicious cycle. I didn't know what to do or where to go. Eventually, I was able to make a plan and get out for good. Life was physically better. Overwhelming poverty, shame, and unfamiliarity took longer to overcome, but it IS possible.

Dr. Becca and Jessa paint what the Stages of Change look like in real life from their own experiences and the many, many people they've served. This book was birthed out of their passion for helping those trapped in horrible situations and abusive relationships. You will begin to grasp that you're not alone.

You'll see the how the authors have beautifully woven story with facts and support. It paints a real example of the stages we all go through when trying to escape our trafficking situations, in all their various forms. For me, I was targeted and groomed by a boyfriend who ended up being a pimp. For you, it might be that you were raised in a family that used, abused, and sold you—a family that should have loved, nurtured, and protected you. For some of you, perhaps gang involvement required you to bring in money for the "family" by providing sexual services to strangers. Perhaps you have been in an explosive relationship where you had to give in and do things that were against your values or comfort level.

Leaving the Life engages you in a story much like our own, encourages you to consider other options, and empowers you to dream of a different, better life.

Rebecca Bender
Founder and CEO, Rebecca Bender Initiative
and Elevate Academy
Survivor Leader, Author and Subject Matter Expert

Introduction

Beware of relationships that:
Focus on sex and not safety
Involve more lust than love
Seem more abusive than affectionate
View you as property rather than view you properly

Why Read This Book?

If you are in or have ever been in a tough and complicated situation or relationship, this book is for you.

It is about Elisa's journey and may be about your journey as well. Although Elisa's story may be different than yours, you might find many similarities – vulnerabilities, abuse, regretted decisions, bad relationships, drugs, violence, emotional turmoil, fear, anger, self-blame, self-hatred and more.

Elisa's story is that of a female in an abusive and coercive situation. This book, however, is for anyone who has experienced abuse, violence and exploitation, regardless of gender, age, ethnicity, race or religion.

We believe both you and your story are important.

Our desire is that this book will help you begin to see yourself and your options differently. Although choice is hard at times, especially if people in the past have used it against you, we want to encourage you to make your own decisions and live your own life. We want to help you see that there can be freedom from violent relationships and exploitation. We want to come alongside you in this process of making positive changes.

Along with Elisa's story, we've included thoughts and feelings shared by others who have walked a similar journey. Even though your story is different than Elisa's, most of what she thinks, feels, fears and doubts are likely the same.

Each chapter includes part of **Elisa's Story**. The **Reflections** that follow provide helpful information on a variety of topics. **Survivor Sharing** is where others (who have walked the path of hard relationships) share their thoughts. Lastly, **Your Story** asks questions to help you process what you are learning. You can decide whether or not to write down your answers or just think about them.

Feel free to mark the book up, write in the margins, fill in the blanks or underline and highlight the parts that are particularly meaningful to you and your situation.

Note: If it's not safe to have a copy of the book, ask for a digital version (leavingthelife.org).

The Process of Change

You may be asking, "Am I crazy? Am I normal?" If so, you are not alone. Most of those in these complicated relationships ask themselves the same questions. In fact, after hearing about the Stages of Change, most recognize their own experience and let out an emotional sigh of relief, "Oh, I *am* normal!"

The Stages of Change model* identifies five stages that people experience as they gradually move away from harmful situations (behaviors, relationships, addictions, lifestyles) to healthy ones (*from the Transtheoretical model of behavior change). Here's a brief summary, which includes an additional, common last stage:

- **Precontemplation:** You're not ready or willing to change your situation (habit, relationship, behavior &/or lifestyle)
- **Contemplation:** You begin to acknowledge that there's a problem and think about the possibility of changing your situation

- **Preparation:** You begin planning how to change your situation
- **Action:** You take action to change your situation
- **Maintenance:** You are working on building a new life and strengthening your resolve to not return to the former negative, unwanted situation
- **Recycle / Relapse → Preparation → Action → Maintenance:** You returned to your unhealthy situation but are making plans once again to leave and return to working on building a better life, free from the harmful situation

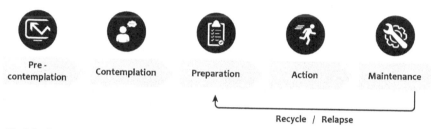

Self-Care

As you read this book, it is vital that you practice some self-care; that is, do things that help you feel better and stronger. Our favorite self-care includes wrapping up in a blanket, listening to calming music, washing our faces with warm water, getting outside, or drinking a favorite hot drink. For others, it might be taking a walk, a bath or a shower, or, drawing or doodling. If you can't think of anything, try something from our list. As you get to know yourself, make your own self-care list to use when feeling overwhelmed. It may take time, but eventually, you'll learn what helps you feel safe and secure.

Contrary to what you may have been told or what you may believe, help and hope are available. There are people who care and programs to help. Not everyone wants to exploit and use you. Do not believe the lies that say otherwise. You can face the challenges and needed changes in your own life. We are here cheering you on. We believe in you!

About the Authors

As a psychologist, Dr. Becca has spent many years working with victims of sexual abuse and exploitation. She focuses on the trauma recovery process, assisting these amazing survivors on their journey of emotional healing.

Jessa's perspective is invaluable and personal. As a survivor of familial and pimp-controlled sexual exploitation as well as labor trafficking, Jessa understands the difficulty and challenge of leaving the Life. She has been there, knows how hard the recovery process is, and knows the beauty of freedom. Jessa has taken the hard things she has experienced and used these to propel her to complete a Master of Clinical Mental Health Counseling and to co-found BridgeHope, an anti-trafficking nonprofit organization.

Karalyn, an exceptional reader-writer, adds the compelling story, developed from real-life people and situations, that invites us into the heart and mind of Elisa.

Together, Becca, Jessa, and Karalyn are a unique team—a helper, a survivor, and a writer—all who want to encourage you to leave The Life in order to enjoy real life. These justice-seekers and heart-helpers long to help you heal and find freedom.

CHAPTER 1

Elisa

My life and my pain are one and the same.

Here we begin Elisa's story. It might be overwhelming and it might be familiar. Take breaks if needed. Do self-care as needed, whether wrapping in a blanket, sipping tea, listening to calming music, going for a walk or run, or taking a bath or a shower. But do keep reading – all of Elisa's story. The end is so worth reading.

Elisa's Story

As a child, I saw myself as a protector.

When my sister Emelia, five years my junior, first came home from the hospital, my mother looked me square in the eyes and told me: "This is Emmy, you will take care of her and love her and make sure nobody hurts her." I nodded my head fervently, already in love with little Emmy, and knowing that when my mother said "nobody," she actually meant my father.

For the next four years, until our dad finally left, it was my job to hide Emmy in the bathroom every time he came home drunk, or every time he would lose his temper with our mom. I would grab Emmy's hand and rush her into the bathroom. I would tell her to sing her favorite song – "Puff The Magic Dragon" – and wait for me to come get her. I would then shut the door and go sneak behind the fridge where I would watch my dad throw things at my mom, hit her, or pin her down. Sometimes my dad would see me and it would bring him back to himself. Other times he was so far gone that he would reach for me and threaten to hurt me. Only once did he actually strike me.

When I was nine, my dad finally left. Although on one hand I felt relief, on the other, I simply felt incredibly alone. My mom had to start working two jobs, so my grandmother moved in. My grandmother, the wonderful old lady that she was, was also useless at everything except waking us up in the morning and then watching TV for the rest of the day.

Every morning I would dress Emmy, pack her lunch, and ride with her on the subway until we reached her school. After dropping her off in her classroom, I would then run the twelve blocks to my own school and arrive late every day. I never minded the frequent lunch detentions for my tardiness.

I had a few close friends at school but I never hung out with them outside of school. They didn't understand why, but that was OK. While my friends went to the mall or to one another's houses, I would walk Emmy home from school each day and fix us a snack. I would make sure she did her homework and then make her read for an hour. Mom was always working, and by this time, Grandma was sick and always sleeping, so it was left to me to take care of Emmy.

There was a day when I was thirteen that changed everything for me. Emmy was at a friend's house, so it was just me at our apartment that afternoon. I don't remember how it happened exactly, but somehow I ended up in our neighbor's apartment next door. The son, Rudy, who was seventeen at the time, was there alone. Rudy and I were sitting on the couch and he was showing me some CDs from his music collection. I distinctly remember the song "Back in Black" by AC/DC playing when his hand first started caressing my thigh.

It started with kissing, which was exhilarating to me because I had never been kissed before. His hand started reaching under my shirt, which I was less OK with, but I didn't say anything. When his hand traveled inside my jeans, I tried to pull away.

"No," I said, trying to sit up. He pushed me down on the couch and used his body weight to keep me there.

"Come on, Elisa, you know you want this."

"No," I said again, trying to squirm out from under him. Rudy just laughed.

He pinned my shoulders down with his as he lifted his hips up to unbutton his jeans and wiggle out of both his pants and his underwear. He quickly pulled my jeans and underwear down. I froze and felt powerless. I closed my eyes for what happened next.

When it was over, I lay on his couch with just my bra on and stared up at the ceiling. I couldn't move. I didn't know how to feel, let alone what to feel.

"You should probably go home," Rudy said as he started pulling on his jeans. "Don't want your mama to worry." He gave me a wink that made my stomach twist. Suddenly, I jumped up and starting quickly pulling my clothes on. Once on I headed straight for the door, not looking back as I slammed it behind me and ran into my own apartment next door.

I stood just inside our apartment for a few moments, looking around at the empty rooms and taking deep breaths in an effort to calm myself. A moment later I was rushing to the bathroom and throwing up into the toilet. After I finished vomiting, I sat there next to the toilet bowl and cried.

I avoided Rudy after that day, in fact, I avoided everyone after that day. I stopped talking to my friends at school and stopped even talking to my mother in the evenings.

I didn't know who I was. I felt so empty and broken inside. Somehow, Rudy had stripped me of everything I thought I was.

Except Emmy's protector.

While I stopped talking to and drew back from others, I pushed myself forward even more into Emmy's life. I swore to myself that nothing like what had happened to me would ever happen to Emmy. In the afternoons I would ignore my own homework and work with Emmy on hers, testing her and tutoring her. I stopped letting her go on playdates, terrified of what would happen to her if I wasn't there to protect her.

———————

Life carried on this way until I was fifteen, when our mother remarried a man named Bill.

Bill, while he had dated my mother for almost a year, had been very respectful and kind, always bringing us gifts and taking the time to get to know Emmy and me. I never really opened up to Bill, as I was barely speaking to my mother at this point, but I could tell that he made our mom happy and he never became violent with her.

A few months into their marriage, our mom started taking the night shift at her job. Bill, who worked days at his own job, would come home around six every night and it was I who would make dinner for him, Emmy, Grams and myself.

I can remember the first night it happened. Bill had had too much to drink, and I woke up to him entering my bedroom late at night. All the lights in the house were out, and at first I thought it was Emmy coming into my room.

Bill closed the door behind him. I sat up in bed.

"What's going on?" I asked, still groggy from sleep.

"Shh." Bill put his hand over my mouth. "We don't want to make too much noise."

I tried to shake his hand away. I was still confused as to what was going on.

I managed to swat his hand away but a second later it was replaced with his slimy lips.

I was so shocked that it took me a few seconds to try and push him away. "What the hell are you doing?" I said in a loud voice. Bill's hand went to my mouth again, this time more forcefully, and it drowned out the protests I was making.

"Come on, Elisa. Don't make this difficult," Bill said. He pushed my head down on my pillow and climbed on top of me, pinning me down. I tried to scream but his hand blocked the noise. I bit his hand.

Bill swore, taking his hand away. I started to scream, but soon found my pillow pushing into my face. I couldn't see him, but I soon felt his breath at my ear.

"Elisa, I want you, but if you're going to make this difficult, your sister is right down the hall and I wouldn't mind her at all."

Suddenly my body froze. Emmy. No, this could never happen to her.

"That's right," Bill whispered. "If you shut up, then you save your sister."

I held still. He slowly lifted the pillow from my face and threw it on the ground. He stood up and stared at me for a moment. I prayed to God that he would just leave me alone.

I closed my eyes as soon as I heard him unzipping his jeans. I could hear him undressing.

"Open your eyes," he commanded. I kept them closed.

His hand slapped across my face, leaving a burning heat behind. "Open your eyes," he said through clenched teeth.

I opened my eyes and looked at him. He was naked.

"Good," he said. "Now take off your clothes."

———————

The next morning, I had two blissful seconds before I remembered what had happened. But then it hit me and I felt my stomach twisting. I went and checked on Emmy right away. She was just getting up. She smiled at me.

"Hey, Elisa!" she said as I opened her door. I stood in the doorframe for a few seconds and studied her, trying to determine if anything had happened to her.

She looked at me inquisitively. "What's up?" she asked, giving me a look telling me I was acting crazy. *She's alright.*

"Nothing!" I said, trying to be cheerful. "Just making sure you're up." I gave the only smile I could muster and walked away.

That night I stayed awake in bed, praying and praying that Bill wouldn't come.

He did though.

He came almost every night for the next two years.

Bill always reminded me that I was a good big sister, and that because I didn't make a sound or say anything, I was protecting my sister.

And I was. Emmy was the only reason I didn't scream. She was the only reason, in those darker moments, that I didn't slit my wrists. The only reason I avoided bridges and my never-ending dream to jump off of them and fly away.

Emmy thrived. She did well in school and I made her apply for a scholarship to a boarding school in Connecticut.

The day Emmy received her letter of acceptance I burst into tears. Emmy was getting out! If she went to Connecticut, then she would be free of this horrible apartment and horrible city.

I took the train up with her and helped her move into her dorm. She had a wonderful roommate named Erika. Before I left I gave her one last talk. I told her not to have any sex, and if she even thought about it, to talk to me first. I told her to do well in school and pour her heart into her studies. I told her to find something she was passionate about and pursue it. I told her to try every sport until she found one she loved. I told her to make dozens of friends, to always be herself, and to never let anyone take advantage of her. And lastly, I told her I loved her more than anything.

I cried the whole train ride back. Emmy was safe. I knew I had protected her by getting her out, but I also felt helpless because I wasn't going to be able to see her or protect her every day.

Somehow, I thought that with getting Emmy out, Bill would lose his leverage over me. But he still came into my room nearly every night and now said that he would pull Emmy out of school if I said anything.

While my own nightmare continued, I found comfort knowing that Emmy was far away. I had learned long ago how to shut my mind off, my feelings off, when Bill came to visit my room. In those moments when Bill was on top of me, inside of me, I imagined Emmy at her school, learning and loving, and I found a way to get through those moments of despair. I found a way to be happy.

———————

I was nearly eighteen when I met AJ. It was January and Emmy had just gone back for her second semester. My mom and Bill were having problems, and every day I would pray on my walk to school that she would just kick him out and that the nightmare would end.

I started going to parties more often and even acquired a fake ID so I could get into bars. I was at a club one night and stepped outside for a few minutes to clear my head from all the alcohol, smoke, and dancing.

I was having a strange moment of clarity, thinking about me, my life and my future when someone sat down on the curb next to me. I looked up to see a handsome man, probably a few years older than me. I smiled at him.

"You look familiar," he said, studying my features. "Do you work at Harvey's?" Harvey's was a bar a few blocks away. No, I didn't work there – I was underage – but I was flattered that he thought I was older.

I shook my head.

"Damn," he said. "I don't know where from then."

I shrugged my shoulders and continued to smile up at him.

"I'm AJ," he said, stretching out his hand. I shook it.

"I'm Elisa," I responded.

"That's an exotic-sounding name. How do you spell it?"

"E, L, I, S, A."

"Well, Elisa, with the pretty name, what are you doing out here all by yourself?" he inquired, looking down into my eyes.

"Escaping," I responded.

"Oh, I see," he said and took my left hand in both of his. "Would you like some company as you escape? Or maybe someone to help you escape?"

I smiled and nodded my head as he stood up and pulled me up after him.

"Well, off we go on a new adventure then." He smiled at me and wrapped my hand in his as we walked away from the club.

I woke up in AJ's apartment the next morning. I couldn't remember much from the night before. I sat up in bed just as AJ entered the room with a tray full of breakfast.

"Morning, sunshine." AJ put the tray down beside me on the bed and reached over it to give me a quick kiss on the mouth.

He must have noticed my confused expression. "You don't remember much, do you?" I shook my head, not sure I wanted to know either.

"Well" – he started explaining – "we went to a bar and chatted over drinks. You told me about school and Emmy and how you don't know what you're going to do after you graduate in a few months. I told you about my job as a mechanic and that I'm twenty-four and that I think you're very beautiful." He smiled at me. "I was going to walk you home, but you said you didn't want to go to that place, so I brought you here."

I looked around at the room and the bed that I was currently sitting in, unsure.

"Nothing happened," he laughed. "Well," he leaned his face in close to mine, "Nothing more than a few sweet kisses." He gave me a small kiss then and his lips felt different than any that had kissed me before. They were gentle, soft, and probing. Not aggressive.

I found myself leaning into his kiss and kissing him back. It was a new sensation, kissing someone who I actually wanted to kiss. A fire started in my belly, and not the usual twist of disgust that burned there.

AJ was the first to pull away. I breathed heavily, reveling in this new experience.

AJ laughed. "Wow," he said, smiling at me.

I smiled back at him. "Wow."

I fell for AJ pretty quickly. He was so different from the other men I had known in my life. He brought me flowers some days after school and always left notes and funny little inappropriate jokes for me to find. AJ's apartment became my sanctuary, where I hid from Bill and where I felt safe.

One night after we had sex for the first time, my first real time, I cried. AJ comforted me and I told him about Bill. AJ was silent when I told him. He stayed silent for many long moments.

"Can I kill him?" he asked in all seriousness.

I looked at him for a few moments. "No," I shook my head. I snuggled up to him. "Just keep me safe."

We stayed there a few minutes together before AJ spoke up again. "Please don't go back there." He lifted his head to look down on me. "Move in with me. I'll keep you safe here with me."

And so AJ and I moved in together. At first, it was so freeing. AJ was my protector. I had always been the protector, never been protected, and it was so wonderful to finally have someone looking after me.

When I left home I told my mom where she could find me and how to contact me. I told her I was leaving because I wasn't going to live under the same roof as Bill. Although I didn't tell her why, I'm sure she understood though. I also told her that if she took Emmy out of school, I would take Emmy away and we would never speak to her again. I didn't say a word to Bill as I left.

For the first few months at AJ's, it was mostly just the two of us. But as soon as I graduated and started looking for a job, more and more of AJ's friends started to hang around.

It was around this time that I realized AJ was more than just a mechanic. Many of the individuals who came to our apartment came for drugs, and AJ readily supplied them – for a cost.

I had trouble finding a job. Some days, instead of going out and trying, AJ would say: "You can stay home, Elisa. Take some of this, it'll help you relax and get you in a better place. You can look tomorrow."

Soon I stopped looking for a job.

AJ used to host parties at our apartment. There would be twenty or so people, most of them high on one thing or another. I used to try and play hostess. AJ would call them "our parties" and "our apartment," and so I tried to fit into the role of hostess and see to everything.

The first time I walked in on AJ with another girl was at one of these parties.

I had been out buying more beer and when I came back, I couldn't find AJ. Well, I soon found him in our bedroom. When they saw me walk in, they stopped. AJ stood up but the girl stayed on the bed and looked almost bored.

"You can go," AJ said to the girl. She stood up and starting walking out the door.

"See you soon," she said to me on her way out. I didn't bother to wonder at her meaning as I turned to AJ.

"What the hell?" I wanted to scream it, but it came out as a whisper.

"I'm sorry, baby," AJ said, walking toward me and pulling me down to sit next to him on the bed. "I'm so sorry." He looked into my eyes. "I am so high right now." I went to pull my hand away. "But come on, you know it's you. You know I love you. You're my Elisa. We're going to grow old together." He lifted my chin up so I would look into his eyes. "You know I love you. Don't you love me?"

I sighed. "Yes, of course I love you."

AJ bought me many apology gifts after the first time it happened. He bought less after the second time.

The third time I found AJ with another trashy-looking girl at one of his little get-togethers, I started crying. "Why?" I asked. "Why do you do this?"

AJ was silent for a moment. "Elisa, I love you, but I also get frustrated with you. You sit around here all day high on my drugs and don't work or pay rent." His voice rose. "For God's sake, can't you contribute to our rent or something?" When he was finished yelling at me, he stormed out of the room. I was left to cry by myself.

At the next party, instead of acting the hostess, I got high instead. was dreading what I would find if I went into the bedroom.

AJ and my interactions had been different ever since the last party. He now openly criticized me when I stayed home and got high. Things were distant. I had tried to talk to him, but every time I started talking he would tell me to shut up and "take off my clothes."

The first time he said this I hesitated and AJ threw me down onto the bed. "Take off your clothes," he said as he crawled onto the bed after me. AJ was rough and I remember thinking while we were in the middle of it, *Wait, who is this?* Romantic AJ, my protector, seemed to have disappeared.

But we couldn't break up. I wouldn't let that happen. I needed AJ. I couldn't go home; I couldn't get a job or pay rent anywhere.

AJ had saved me. I couldn't lose him.

So at that next party, I couldn't take finding him with another girl, couldn't care and make a big deal about it. I wouldn't give AJ an excuse to kick me out. To stop loving me.

At some point, AJ came and found me on the couch next to Aiden, one of his friends.

"Elisa, come with me." He held out his hand and pulled me up off the couch. He walked me down the hall toward the bedroom. We stopped just outside the door.

"Elisa," he said, "I need your help." I looked up at him.

"What do you need?" I asked.

"We're low on rent and I need money. Can you help us out?"

"How?" I asked, unsure of what I could do.

AJ sighed before speaking, he looked hesitant. "James said he'd give me a hundred bucks if you have sex with him."

"What?" I asked, alarmed and recoiling from him.

AJ caught my hand and looked into my eyes. "Please, Elisa, this is the only way." I looked at him like he was crazy.

"You loved your sister enough to do it for her. Don't you love me enough too?"

His words stung. But he was right, I did love him. Did I love him enough?

I can't lose him.

"OK," I said hesitantly. A smile spread across AJ's face.

"Thank you, baby. You have no idea how much I love you for this." He gave me a quick peck on the lips. "I'll be right on the other side of this door."

I looked at the door to our bedroom. James was waiting on the other side. I looked up at AJ one more time.

"I love you, baby," he said, his eyes almost twinkling.

I took a deep breath and then pushed open the door. (To be continued ...)

———

Reflections

Reading this story most likely has brought up a lot of emotions for you; it did for us. Emotions like anger, fear, confusion, guilt, shame, and sadness. Although it might be hard to read, we want you to know that it is OK to feel what you are feeling. Your emotions are real and they are important. This IS a sad, horrible story – and similar to that of many others who have been abused.

Just like Elisa and possibly you, far too many adults and young children have experienced neglect, physical abuse, assault and unwanted sexual encounters. For example, it's possible that you were forcefully hurt, touched in ways that made you feel uncomfortable, physically mistreated, and belittled repeatedly or at some point in your life. That is called abuse. Physical abuse or assault is bodily harm inflicted on you by another person. Emotional abuse occurs when someone says horrible degrading, demeaning things about us. Sexual abuse is unwanted sexual activities with a minor, such as when Bill and Rudy forced themselves on Elisa, and it is also sexual assault when an unwanted sexual advancement is made to an adult." If any of these are your experiences, you are not alone! Many, far too many, people have been used, abused and misused, threatened, coerced and manipulated.

We know that the #MeToo movement has opened the door for some individuals to feel safe to speak about the sexual abuse and assault they have experienced. Yet, many of us are still afraid to speak out about our own unwanted sexual experiences because we feel shame, blame, rejection, fear, and self-doubt. And, if our abusers have also threatened to harm us or others, we feel trapped. Just as powerful as the threat of physical harm is that of emotional/mental harm. Fear and shame hold us in bondage, and we end up keeping silent, trying to survive. Elisa was trying to survive and to protect her little sister, Emmy.

Many who've been abused don't even realize that what happened to them would be considered abuse or an assault. If you experienced physical and sexual abuse or assault and didn't know what it was until recently, you aren't alone. It wasn't your fault. This delayed response is normal.

Unfortunately, those who have experienced abuse, especially sexual abuse, are more vulnerable to further and future abuse. We have seen this over and over again with many of the people who we have helped. A recommended book that helps in overcoming the negative effects of abuse is *The Journey to Hope: Overcoming Abuse* (Johnson, 2018, available on Amazon.com).

After people experience abuse, they often carry many unanswered questions. Questions like, *Why did I let this happen? Why me? Why didn't I tell someone? What is wrong with me?* Here are some of the many questions that Elisa and other victims have asked:

- *Why did this happen to me?*
- *What would have happened if I'd told someone?*
- *Why do I feel so responsible for everything that's happened?*
- *Why did my abuser interfere with my life?*
- *Have other people been used and abused by this person?*
- *Did anyone else know about it but just not say anything?*
- *Why didn't someone protect me or see that it was happening?*
- *Do other people feel this way (those who have been treated like this)?*
- *Why did I let it go on so long? What was my biggest fear?*
- *How can I try to forget about what happened?*
- *Am I crazy? Am I just making this up?*
- *Wouldn't it just be easier to end this all (suicide)?*
- *Why do I feel so stupid? Lonely? Powerless?*
- *Is there anything I can do about what happened?*

In addition to the many questions that victims ask, there are also many negative thoughts and feelings of self-blaming, including:

Thoughts

- I should have known better.
- I should have tried harder.
- I should have done something differently.
- It's my fault.

- I'm worthless (stupid, dirty, hopeless).
- Others can't find out.
- I can't do anything right.
- He says he loves me but ...

Feelings

- *Guilt, self-blaming*
- *Shame-filled*
- *Fearful (of others finding out, of harm)*
- *Betrayed*

- *Angry (mostly at myself)*
- *Hopeless, powerless*
- *Confused, ambivalent*

When the questions, self-blame, self-hatred and anger are left unanswered or unchallenged, victims of abuse and rape often seek ways to deaden the pain and deal with the negative thoughts and feelings. Although you will have your own unique responses and reactions, generally one responds to abuse with unhealthy relationships and self-destructive behaviors such as cutting, entering into another abusive relationship, eating disorders, drugs, addictions, and anything else that deadens the pain.

Survivor Sharing

(Thoughts shared in this section come from people who have been through tough, terrible, traumatic things.)

As a victim, you have no voice. If I could have had a platform with no risk, this is what I would have screamed aloud:

- *Leave me alone! Just leave me alone!*

- *What did I ever do to you? Am I really so horrible? Such a burden?*

- *Why do you let me live? When are you going to kill me already?*

- *I am not a belonging.*

- *I am not an object to owned, traded, won, dressed up, manipulated or exploited.*

- *I am not for sale, rent, trade or barter.*

- *You're supposed to love me, what the hell happened?*

- *I'm too tired, I'm exhausted, I'm in pain*

- *What did I do wrong?*

- *I just want a normal life. This is too hard.*

- *No. Stop. Why?*

9 to 20 Blog, February, 2012

- *By the time my boyfriend asked me to sleep with his friends to make us money, I'd already been broken in by my uncle when I was young.*

Anonymous

- *Even though I hated having sex with random guys off the street, I'd been doing it for years at drug parties. I wanted to deaden the pain I felt inside from when my stepdad first sexually abused me.*

Anonymous

- *I can't help but think of all the thousands of girls looking for love in all the wrong places. So, so many girls end up in pornography or prostitution not because some mean guy literally kidnapped them. More often it's a (fake) boyfriend who convinced her that she should do him a favor if "she really loves him." This might sound foolish, but when you're desperate for affection and care, or desperate for a way to financially provide, this seems anything but foolish ... this seems to make perfect sense.*

  9to20 Blog, February, 2012

Your Story

Friend, maybe your story is a bit like Elisa's in the ways that you have experienced abuse and assault, and as a result, you have been involved in some destructive behaviors and harmful relationships. Please keep reading ... Elisa's story continues, as does yours. As you process your story, here are several questions for you to answer to understand more about who you are and the ways that the past has affected you.

Have you like other abuse victims ...

→ blamed yourself for what happened?

→ not told anyone because you were scared or ashamed?

→ done harmful things to deaden your pain?

Thoughts, Feelings, Reflections and/or Doodles

CHAPTER 2

AJ

Survival wasn't figuring out how to live in the woods,
it was figuring out how to stay alive in The Game.

Elisa's Story

Fortunately, James was really quick. After he finished, I took a shower and went back into the room to join the party. AJ smiled at me and it made some of the disgust I felt dissolve away. He was happy, which made me happy.

As time went on, I became more dependent on AJ for everything. He was the center of my life. Even though there was so much shit taking place, including being asked multiple times over the next few weeks to have sex with other guys at the parties, I learned to put up with it because we needed the money. It might not make sense to you, but it was worth it to me when it came to the moments that he was really sweet and loving. Besides, the drugs helped me to numb the pain.

Now it was commonplace for him to have multiple guys waiting to be with me. The only kind of host that I had become was a host who invited people into my body with a fake smile pulling at my lips. I was feeling trapped and my vagina was burning all the time.

I still would catch him with other girls once in a while, but I learned to put up with it. He would repeatedly tell me that I was his favorite and then he would woo me back to him – always ending with a tender sexual encounter, which always made me sigh in relief as the feeling of safety returned.

So, one day when he told me he had a house of other girls like me who he had helped and that they were now contributing to the lifestyle and parties that we had, I was shocked and hurt. Yet, I was comforted to know that I was his number one and that none of them were allowed to sleep over at his apartment. Just me.

The first time I went to this house, I was there for only one night. The next time he took me there it was for three nights, followed by a week. AJ told me that I didn't belong there and that it was only temporary. I had to believe him and I did believe him. If I didn't, I would go crazy. But the number of days at the house with the other girls kept getting longer and harder to survive.

"Elisa, Jimmy called for you. He has time this afternoon and wants to know if you'll meet him." Veronica stepped out of the bathroom in just a towel. She was tall and see-your-ribs skinny. She was normally always so high that I was surprised she was able to take a message and relay it to me now. I stared at her for a few seconds, taking in her sober self.

"Do you have something special today?" I asked bluntly.

Veronica gave me a sassy smile. "Why, yes, I do." She stuck her tongue out at me. She then paused and observed me for a few moments before speaking again, this time in a more serious tone. "AJ is taking me to see my son today."

It took a few moments for me to understand what she was saying. A sudden fear bubbled up in my stomach. "Who's the father?" The words spilled out of my mouth before I could contain them.

Veronica smirked. "Don't worry, it's not AJ." She dropped the towel and started to pull on a dress over her breakable frame. Her eyes found mine again before she spoke. "It was an old friend of AJ's. They live upstate and I'm only allowed to see my son every few months, and only if I can pay my way up there."

I stared at Veronica as she continued to get ready for her big day. I watched the way she took time to brush out her hair and put in earrings, taking the few extra moments she would usually never bother with. I stared at her putting in so much effort, and while her appearance changed before my eyes, so did my perception of her.

Veronica had a child.

I looked around at the other beds in our room, and thought about the other rooms in this house filled with girls AJ helped. Did they have kids? Was AJ the father of any of *their* children? What kind of secrets were all of them hiding?

My heart started to beat a little faster as I became more and more anxious.

What if AJ did have kids with any of them? Would that make them more important to him?

No, *Elisa*, I tried to reassure myself. *He said he loves you. You've spent three nights at his apartment this week! When was the last time anyone else got to sleep in his bed?*

My heart continued to pound faster and faster.

I realized I hadn't been high since late last night and it was almost midday. That's why I was getting so anxious.

I needed to call Jimmy and say I could meet him at his place. But I knew I wouldn't do as well or get any kind of tip if I didn't get high right now.

And after Jimmy's, I could go and deliver the money to AJ. I'd have to wear something really sexy too. If I kept surprising him with money and sex, AJ wouldn't be able to stop loving me. Maybe he'd even invite me to move in with him again.

I looked in my stash and let out a sigh of relief just at the thought of releasing all this anxiety into my high.

There was no way AJ didn't love me, not after all I do for him. (To be continued ...)

Reflections

It is possible, that just like Elisa, you might be thinking that you are OK and that your *boyfriend* is good to you, that he loves you and understands you in ways that no one else can. You might be thinking that you don't have any problems and that you don't need any help. It is possible that you and your *boyfriend* have future dreams together. Even though you might have a lot of unspoken fears and questions, you are not ready to make a change yet. That's understandable. You want to hold out hope that things will get better, that the good in your partner will overcome the bad that you are experiencing. You are afraid that no one else would or could ever love you, especially if they knew about you and what you've done. You just aren't ready to think about leaving.

Oftentimes sexual abuse and rape create vulnerabilities that can lead to the person being used by other people, sometimes resulting in sexual exploitation and trafficking.

Although we have already discussed what sexual abuse and assault are, we have not yet discussed sexual exploitation, prostitution, and trafficking. Sex trafficking is the "action of recruitment, transportation, and harboring of a person through improper means such as force, fraud, and coercion for the improper purpose of forced labor and sexual exploitation" (TVPA). In other words, it is when someone forces you or talks you into doing sex acts for their profit and gain (for example, pornography, stripping, and sex for drugs, money, or other benefits).

Maybe you are in a relationship like Elisa or maybe you are caught in a toxic family situation with abuse and exploitation. You'd like it to stop but don't know how and wonder if it is even possible.

After I started to process the ongoing sexual abuse, violence, and exploitation I had experienced, I struggled to make sense of my world. I felt like I didn't fit in. The only place that I could experience acceptance was with others who had experienced hardships similar to mine.

You've probably tried to convince yourself of the following when life is overwhelming and you feel used and confused:

- *I'm OK.*
- *I love him and he loves me.*
- *Others don't understand.*
- *I don't have a problem. I don't need any help.*
- *We have wonderful future plans.*
- *It's not perfect but no relationship is.*
- *I don't want to change but even if I wanted to, I don't think I could.*

When we are in these terrible situations, we spend so much energy convincing ourselves that we will be OK and that things will get better. Our dreams often fade away or are used against us. It might be helpful for you to ask yourself these questions (take time to really think about your answers):

→ What do I like/not like about my life?

→ What dreams have I had?

→ What do I wish could be different?

If you could start all over again, what would you do?

What were your plans before all of this (the horrible things) happened?

I wanted to go to training school to become a _____

I wanted to pursue my dream to become a _____

____I planned to go to college.

____I'd hoped to travel a lot.

____I wanted to get married and have children.

____I wanted to help others.

____I wanted to work with animals.

____Other: _____.

One dream that we all have is to be loved. It's a built-in human need. It's normal and it's OK to want love. The problem is when you "look for love in all the wrong places." Love is good and life-giving. If a relationship is negative, demanding and demeaning – that's not real, true love.

When a relationship becomes abusive and violent, you need to get out. If you stay, you allow the other person to compromise what you believe, who you are and your hopes and dreams.

Survivor Sharing

(Thoughts shared in this section come from people who have been through tough, terrible, traumatic things.)

When others were asked, "When did you first think about leaving?" here are some of their answers:

- *I didn't think it was possible, so I never really thought about it.*

- *When I began getting beaten up.*

- *I was born into it and just figured why bother trying to leave.*

- *Never, I didn't think I could have any other kind of life.*

- *I would think a lot about getting out by couldn't figure out the when, where and how to do it.*

- *When I started questioning if he really loved me.*

- *Right away.*

- *All the time.*

I often ask ...

> *Why me? Can my life get better, or is this it? Why the hell did I do it? What was I thinking?*

I often wonder ...

> *Am I a lost soul? Will I ever feel peace? Can I ever be set free?*

I wish I could ...

> *Choose a different path. Start all over again. Change it all. Be normal. Undo all of the hurt.*

What would have happened if I didn't get out? Why did it take me so long to get out?

I've been told so many lies – I've begun to believe them.
I've told so many lies – I've begun to believe them.
I tell lies to myself – I've begun to believe them.
I don't know what's true and what's a lie anymore.

Your Story

→ Have you ever thought about leaving?

→ What lies have you told yourself to convince you that everything is OK?

Thoughts, Feelings, Reflections and/or Doodles

CHAPTER 3

The Apartment

I'm questioning my decisions ... I'm questioning my life!

Elisa's Story

"Did AJ hit you again?"

I had barely stepped inside the door before Mary looked up from her trip on the couch and saw the bruising around my eye.

"No, of course not," I said, reaching up to touch just under my eye. It was tender under my fingers.

"Are you sure? Looks like it." Mary just continued to stare at me. It made me feel uncomfortable.

"It was my own fault," I said. "I didn't get a very big tip last night. And I passed out before he could send me somewhere else." Mary just nodded as if to say, "Been there, done that." Then as she seemed to gaze into space, she said out loud, "It happens."

I walked to my room, finding it empty, and sat on the end of my bed.

AJ had now hit me six times.

I reached into my bag and pulled out some of my stash, which AJ had given to me to apologize for hitting me.

See, he does care, I told myself. I soon lost myself to my high.

Emmy called me yesterday. I had seen her the few times she came home last summer. She had stayed the night at AJ's apartment with me. She had called me and asked if I was coming home for Christmas. I didn't know what to say.

Would AJ let me go? He hadn't let me go to my grandma's funeral.

Would I ever see Emmy again?

Not that you want her to see you like this.

I looked over at the older man who was sleeping beside me in the bed. He paid me extra to sleep over for the night. Just before falling asleep, he whispered in my ear, "You remind me of my daughter." I cringed inside and wished I'd never heard it. I was so glad that I wasn't his daughter.

I slowly eased my way up from the bed and made my way to the bathroom. I turned on the light and closed the door behind me.

I stared at the girl in the mirror. Her face seemed thin and almost hollow. Her eyes had circles around them and looked darker than I remembered. I tried to make her smile, but she wasn't able to.

No, Emmy can't see me like this.

When had this even happened? I tried to think back to what had led me to where I was right now, in a strange man's bathroom.

Rudy. Bill. James. AJ.

AJ?

But AJ loved me.

No, a thought pierced through my mind, AJ doesn't love you.

Emmy does though, and she wants to see you.

I knew I didn't want her to see me like this, but I desperately wanted to see her. Maybe I could sneak away tomorrow and see her, just for a little while. Or maybe longer than a little while. Maybe I could run away with Emmy and we could go start over in a new place. New place. New people. New names – a clean slate. I could get sober and find a job.

But Emmy is still in school, you can't take her away from that. And AJ would never let you go. I traced an old bruise that was now just a shadow of yellow around my left eye.

I pushed my face closer to the mirror and looked into my own bloodshot eyes. After a few minutes of staring at them, my vision started to go blurry. I whispered to myself, "I am going to wait this out."

There was a sudden pounding on the door.

"Are you alright in there?" The man's voice sounded scratchy and only a little impatient.

"I'm fine!" I said quickly, tearing my eyes away from my reflection. "I'm coming!"

And my living nightmare continued. (To be continued ...)

Reflections

You might be reading about Elisa and are currently overwhelmed with the reality of her experiences. We are too. We hurt for her and for others who have experienced these kinds of horrors. Yet, Elisa still believes that AJ is good to her most of the time, that he loves her, and that others just don't understand the life that she lives. It also appears that Elisa is scared to leave and doesn't even know where to get help. The unknown of leaving is often more terrifying than the horror of staying because if you stay, you at least know more of what to expect and already have defense mechanisms built up for what you have to deal with there.

We've talked to others who've experienced really hard things like Elisa and are finding themselves trapped in situations where they are being exploited. They've shared that usually when they thought about running, they would change their mind for one reason or another. Many shared that they didn't know where to go and had no idea who to reach out to for help. They continually asked themselves, "Am I really brave enough to leave, to try something else? Do I deserve anything better than this?"

Harmful, negative relationships keep us stuck. These kinds of relationships can manipulate us and our needs, making us feel trapped. We falsely believe that we can't leave because we are indebted to the person and their plans for our lives. Or, others don't leave because they are afraid – of what could happen to them or their loved ones, of being unlovable, or not knowing what to do or where to go.

Every situation is unique, but below are some ways to identify problem relationships:

Older person with a vested interest in you

There might be a large age difference (4–15 years) between you and this other person and they might be super focused on you. (For example, a girl may be between 12–17 years old and the male might be 18–30 years old, or, if late 20s to 30, he might lie and say he is younger).

Good listener

They will be attentive and listen carefully, mainly because they are wanting to learn as much as possible, which can later be used to their benefit. (For example, they want to know what you like/dislike, your dreams, past hurts, relationships, and more).

Empathetic - Seems to genuinely care about you

They will "say the right things" when you share about frustrations or hurts, such as, "I'm sorry you experienced that." Or, "I'd never do that to you." Or, "That's messed up," "Others don't understand you (like I do)."

Agrees with your complaints against parents, school, friends, youth leaders and others in your life

This person will agree with your every complaint against those in authority in your life in an effort to create more division and distance. Their goal is to slowly alienate you from your current life and the people, places and things in it.

Becomes the center or focus of your whole life

Here you begin to spend less time with other friends, family, youth groups or clubs and other commitments. Isolated from others, this person then creates for you a sense of belonging. They want to be the most important person in your life.

Makes lots of promises

This person might want to be your missing protective parental figure, or a romantic, adorable, doting older individual in your life. Often these individuals are looking at your dreams and want to connect you to these dreams. (For example, a man might tell a young girl that he can connect her with her dream of fame as a singer, actress or whatever. He might promise her that they will marry and have that house with the white picket fence and lots of children. He will be her No. 1 fan when she becomes famous. Whatever she dreams of and longs for, he'll promise to provide it.)

Treats you special and gives you nice things

This person begins to buy you things – maybe treats at first, then bigger gifts: clothes, phone, jewelry, electronics – saying that you are special and deserve nice things.

Encourages sexual intimacy – but maybe not at first

This person will be slow to encourage sex and may even say something like, "I want you to be comfortable and want it." But later, intimacy might become more forceful.

Eventually and occasionally shows their anger

Unexpectedly, you will see their anger expressed. It might be scary at first, but this person might cool down and express love as well. This anger might eventually turn to physical violence and then, after that, potentially demeaning and derogatory words follow.

Begins to express a need for money or to "pay them back" for what they have done or given

At first money didn't seem to be an issue, but now, they need money and this person might suggest you work at a strip club, sell drugs, or provide sex for their friends and/or others. You are expected to pay back the money for the gifts or help pay the rent, or ... The trap has been prepared and set.

Begin to force, coerce, threaten or manipulate you, controlling every move

This person will become increasingly controlling, manipulative and violent. Their occasional kindnesses will keep you bonded to them. Although you may hate being prostituted, you might be connected to the person by love or the belief that you can't live without him/her or the lie that no one could or would love you because of what has happened. Or, perhaps you've become dependent on the person for drugs. Your self-esteem has bottomed out. You are in survival mode but you just don't know it yet. You feel trapped and don't see any way out.

Does any of this sound familiar to you and any relationship you have had? Every relationship and situation is unique but ... Please keep reading.

———

Survivor Sharing

(Thoughts shared in this section come from people who have been through tough, terrible, traumatic things.)

- One particular evening ... I just wanted to give up.

  9to20 Blog, August, 2012

- In my younger years, when he would turn me out and force me to go with men I hated for sex, I'd find myself sometimes sneaking into bars on the way home to flirt with other guys. I'd flirt, not to "get" but just so that I could become the ultimate

tease to then turn and walk away. *I wanted to be in control –
scratch that; I was never really in control. I wanted to feel like
my world wasn't out of control.*

9to20 Blog, December, 2011

- I was certain that no one would believe me. *I had been
brainwashed into believing that I was nothing– just a worthless
ho who people would merely look at as a liar, a troubled young
girl, a slut, a crazy person. I felt that there was nowhere I could
turn for help, no one who would understand ... so I stayed. I told
myself to suck it up and bear it. Move on. Go numb. Survive.*

9to20 Blog, October 26, 2011

- I remember thinking a million times if it'd be worth trying an
escape ... *a few times I even did ... but I'd resolve to go back
because there was nowhere else for me to go.*

9to20 Blog, October 26, 2011

- I numbed out. *You have to. Survival means you have to numb
yourself if you're in The Life for any length of time at all.*

Anonymous

Thinking about Leaving?
What's there to think about?
The Pros and Cons –
An early death or an uncertain life

Thinking about Leaving –
The impossible possibilities
The hope-filled hopelessness –
The crazy sanity

> Thinking about Leaving –
> Choosing to believe in something else
> Daring to believe in something more –
> Wanting to believe in something better
>
> Thinking about Leaving? –
> Just Do It!

Your Story

Ask yourself:

What are my reasons for staying? What would be good about staying now? What would be good about staying long-term?

What would be my reasons for leaving? What would be good about leaving now? What would be good about leaving in the long-term, in the future?

→ What keeps me here?

→ Am I happy?

→ When I've been in bad situations in the past, what did I do to change or overcome them?

Thoughts, Feelings, Reflections and/or Doodles

CHAPTER 4

Disconnection

In the beginning, I thought a lot about leaving. That didn't last long.
Then, I figured it was impossible, that this is my life.
Now, when I dream of leaving, I'm overcome with so much fear
that the dream becomes a nightmare.

Elisa's Story

An older lady, probably in her fifties or sixties, approached me yesterday on the street and gave me a card. It was for some dumb shelter for women. She told me to give her a call if I was ever even thinking about getting help. I had the urge to flip her off, but instead just stared at her blankly, thinking, *I am beyond help – no one can help me.*

I kept the card though and forgot about it for most of that day. Today, however, it seemed to be burning a hole in my jeans pocket.

I had a moment this morning when I considered calling it.

Emmy called today asking again if we could meet up when she's in town next week. I told her I wouldn't be able to.

I'm considering changing my number, or at least stop answering her when she calls. It's too dangerous. If AJ knew I wanted to go visit her, he would definitely hurt me and he might hurt her. He made it clear at Christmas that he was my family now and that he didn't approve of my *old family.*

Not that my mom or sister would want to see me now anyway. *Not after who I've become.*

I pulled the card out of my pocket and stared at it for a few moments.

I studied the numbers and memorized them without even realizing it.

I started to pull my phone out but put it back into my pocket thinking, *This is stupid, no one can help me.* Before I knew it, in a daze, I found my hand calling the number and as the phone began to ring, I snapped out of it. Just before I could hang up, I heard a soft, welcoming voice. "Hi, how can I help you?" I quickly hung up, but her voice and what she said continued to ring in my ears. "How can I help? How can I help? How can I help?" *Can I be helped; is help possible?*

But then I remembered, AJ is taking me out tonight. But he was supposed to last week and never did.

I looked at the numbers one more time, before throwing the card down on the sidewalk and walking down the road toward a new client AJ was sending me to.

It has to get better.

"Where's the money?" AJ looked up at me as I entered the room, noticing my empty hand that would normally be carrying his money.

I looked down at my empty hand. "He didn't pay. He said I wasn't what he ordered."

AJ looked at me blankly for a few moments, as if he didn't understand. "So, you didn't service him?"

"No," I said, looking down and shaking my head. "He said he liked blondes."

"So?" AJ said, standing up and walking over to stand in front of me. "You could have seduced him. Sex is sex, whether you're blonde or not."

I made myself look up into his fiery eyes. "I tried, I really did."

AJ's hand slithered out and smacked me across the jaw. I stumbled back and crashed into the wall behind me. "Well, apparently you didn't try hard enough."

He grabbed me by my shoulders and pushed me into the wall again. A pain shot up my back as he slammed me into the hard surface.

"You're going to try harder next time, right?" AJ pinned my shoulders back and was talking a few inches from my face. I turned my head to the side and closed my eyes.

"Look at me, Elisa." I couldn't make myself look at him, but I knew his anger would only grow if I refused him.

I looked up into his eyes. "You will get me my money next time, right? Even if the guy's type is other guys, I always expect my money. If he doesn't take you, go find someone on the street, but—" he pushed his face closer to mine as he finished his sentence, saying the words slowly to emphasize them—"always get me my money."

I stared at him and nodded, my body shaking and my back hurting.

He saw the fear in my eyes and nodded as if only now he was satisfied. But he wasn't, because then he pushed his face that last inch or two and crushed his lips to mine. He pinned my body against the wall and kissed me hard. My body went limp beneath him.

This was the first time I could remember us kissing with me not trying to seduce him, to remind him that he loved me. Instead, this encounter felt new and wrong – something I didn't want. I tried to pull away, turning my head to the side to avoid his open mouth.

He misunderstood my movement and thought I was giving him my neck to kiss. I tried to pull away fully but was slow because of the pain in my back.

"You bitch! You don't want me?"

I shrunk away, but not enough. He swung his fist and hit my left temple with a heavy force. I fell back onto the ground and he climbed on top of me, pinning me down.

"Oh, I'll make you want me." His fist swung again, this time catching me more on my eye. My vision became blurry and then went black. (To be continued ...)

Reflections

As we read Elisa's story, we are beginning to see a trend that the good times are getting less frequent, while the bad times are increasing. Not only is AJ's anger getting worse, but Elisa is constantly being threatened with violence, rape and _____(you fill in the blank). She wants to see her sister Emmy but is scared of what she will think. She is afraid to leave even though she wishes she could.

I have struggled with this in my past as well. For example, when I was being violently exploited, I wondered on a daily basis, *If I could get away, where will I go and what will I do - is this all I am good for.* Then when I was pregnant, I would think about the ways that I wanted my child to have more than violence, and yet, I could not keep him safe. They forced me to have an abortion. Fear daily trapped me into despair. I wanted to change and I desperately hoped that someday I'd be brave enough to leave.

You might be wondering right now, Old bitch, you did leave. This sounds good for you, but who will help me? How will I continue to survive? What about toughing it out, because loyalty equals love, right? It's impossible to leave. And aren't there more negatives to leaving then there are positives? Who will take care of me?

Friend, keep reading ... many other individuals have left The Life. Below are some things that other survivors have shared when they first thought about making a change and leaving, as well as the reasons why they stayed. Stick with us, the story doesn't end here ...

Survivor Sharing

(Thoughts shared in this section come from people who have been through tough, terrible, traumatic things.)

When we asked other survivors, "When did you first think about making a change and leaving?" this is what they shared:

- *After a beating*
- *When I missed my family or my kids*
- *After an especially horrible night with a john or bad trick*
- *When he'd go with someone else and not me*
- *After an overdose*
- *When I had to have an abortion*
- *After he cracked my jaw*
- *When I felt afraid and powerless*
- *When I realized he didn't love me*

When we asked other survivors, "Why did you stay?" this is what they shared:

- *I enjoyed the "glamor"*
- *I thought I was in love*
- *I liked the clothes and things I got*
- *I was afraid of getting hurt*
- *I had nowhere, nothing & no one to go to*
- *My drug addiction*
- *My other addictions (gambling, porn, shoplifting)*
- *I felt like shit – no one else would want me*
- *I believed no one would or could help me*
- *I thought it was my destiny*
- *I was desperate to keep my boyfriend and would do anything*
- *I enjoyed the attention, even though it was disgusting*
- *Since guys would pay to be with me, I thought I must not be so ugly*
- *Fear of failing*
- *Hopelessness*
- *Why did I stay? Absolute idiocy*

Your Story

→ When did you first think about making a change and leaving?

→ Why did you stay?

Thoughts, Feelings, Reflections and/or Doodles

CHAPTER 5

The Hospital

Facing the facts is painful ... but pain can be motivating.

Elisa's Story

When I woke up, I was in a cold hospital room in an uncomfortable bed. AJ was sitting beside me. When he saw my eyes flicker open he said, "Baby, I love you. I am sorry you got hurt." He never left my side.

Although the doctors were helpful and kind, part of me wished that they knew what was going on so they could help me, yet another part of me was glad that they didn't know or suspect. Besides, AJ's attention now might be the turning point in our relationship, to get it back to where it was in the beginning. Maybe it will get better.

As soon as that thought crossed my mind, another shouted, *No, don't fall for that again.* (To be continued ...)

Reflections

Like Elisa, you tell yourself that it will get better, that it's not that bad and that he's just going through a tough time. You want so desperately to believe that it's going to get better, so you convince yourself it will. You live in a delusion, deceiving yourself that you aren't in a living hell. You focus on the things you own, the money you make and the boyfriend who loves you. But you turn a blind eye to the disgusting, despicable, degrading work you have to do and the treatment you receive.

We begin to believe lies about our lives and situations. When the truth is too painful, we convince ourselves that things are OK when they're not. Here's an example of a conversation with two prostituted women – one still being used and abused and one who got out. Notice the difference? One needs so desperately to justify her situation, telling herself that it's not that bad and it's her choice. The other is now able to see more clearly.

Conversation with Two Prostituted Women

Still IN The Life	OUT of The Life
Do/Did you enjoy the work?	
It's OK. It's not so bad.	No! I had to pretend that I did. I was a good actress. I never liked it!
Why do/did you do this type of work?	
To make money for us to have the things we want and because I love him.	I told myself it was because I loved my boyfriend. I'd do anything for him – and I did. Really, I was forced to go out with men, and if I didn't want to, he'd beat me.
Do/Did you have a choice to do this work or not?	
Yes, I do this because my boyfriend and I need to make money to live.	No – I didn't really have a choice. Even though he'd tell me I had a choice, we both knew I didn't. I would be beaten (or my family would be in danger or my child would be taken away) if I didn't do what I was told to do.

Still IN The Life	OUT of The Life

What do/did you have to do?

Just go out with men (some women) and make them feel good.

Sell my soul – at least that's what it felt like. I did some pretty disgusting things. I had to lie a lot too, even to the police and my family. I did some horrible things – to myself and to others. I hurt people. I even got others to join us. I hated what I did.

Could you leave if you wanted to?

Yes, but I didn't want to.

No, not really. It felt like a prison without walls.

Do/Did you get to keep the money you make/made?

He takes care of the money for us. He's better at it.

No, I had to give all of the money to him. He took it and he controlled it.

Why do people pay for sexual services?

Because of their sexual needs or addictions. It's part of life. Some of the tricks are sad or alone. Others just want to have some fun.

Most think it is for sex but I think it's also for a sense of power and control. It's very selfish, getting one's needs met by treating another human being like a purchased product.

To fulfill their fantasies or perverted desires. I had to do whatever the trick wanted, even if it was disgusting and degrading.

BC Johnson, 2015

You may be thinking, *I have no choice. I have no options.* Although you may believe that, it's not true. It's one of those lies. Do you have options? Yes! What are they?

When you find yourself in tough situations, you always have three choices or options:

1. **ACCEPT** the situation you're in: *Give in, Give up*

   Don't try to change the situation. Instead, give in and give up on trying. The result is that you usually end up changing your beliefs and values, compromising who you are, generally in unhealthy, negative ways.

2. **CHANGE** the situation you're in: *Get going, Get working*

   Is change possible? Will the person or the situation be open to changing? Improving? Don't fool yourself into thinking you can change something if it won't budge. But, get going and get working on making needed changes.

If you can't *accept* the situation and if you find you can't *change* it, you may need to ...

3. **LEAVE** the situation: *Get out, Stay out*

   Sometimes the best solution is to leave, to get out of the situation. This is the smart decision when in an unhealthy, destructive, damaging situation. It's not the same as running away from a problem we should face. If we feel trapped or don't see a way out, we need to seek help from others – and not give up.

A friend shared, "This actually mirrors what I was feeling when I decided to leave. I knew one of three things was going to happen. Either

- They were going to kill me (give up),
- I'd have to work up the nerve to kill them (change) or
- I'd try and leave."

Thinking about leaving can be scary. In a true sense, though, your life depends on it. Just because leaving is scary doesn't mean that you shouldn't seriously consider it. In your situation, leaving IS hard, yet leaving IS necessary. It is essential. The physical, mental and emotional cost of a survival-focused life is high.

If you reflect on what has been done to you, what you've been forced to do or what you have done to others, it might help you know which of the above choices to follow – accept, change or leave. While it may be hard to read the list, we're hoping that it helps you to see more clearly what you should do. Take a deep breath and as you read this, ask yourself, "Do I want to continue down this road or not?"

What I've Done or has been Done to Me

Place a check ✓ next to those things you have experienced or done. Add to the list if not included.

_____I lied to my family or a close friend.

_____I had my head or body thrown against a wall.

_____I've been held against my will and not let go.

_____I lied – to the police, judge, social worker ...

_____I had a tattoo put on that I didn't want or choose.

_____I've been burned by a cigarette (or something else) by someone else.

_____I've been whipped with a belt, rope, whip ...

_____I've been deprived of food.

_____I've had sex with disgusting men and women.

_____I've worn seductive clothes and uncomfortable high heel shoes – even in winter.

_____I've been raped.

_____I've been gang-raped.

_____I've done sexual things with animals.

_____I've been held down while others did sexual things to me.

_____I've not known where I was (what city or state).

_____I had orgy sex (several people together at the same time).

_____I've taken heavy drugs and/or been high for days.

_____I've stolen food.

_____I've stolen things – electronics, jewelry ...

_____I've stolen drugs.

_____I had sex for money.

_____I had sex for drugs.

_____I had sex to not get in trouble.

_____I had sex in exchange for food and/or a place to stay/sleep.

_____I held someone down while others raped her/him.

_____I beat someone up.

_____I injured someone with an object: knife, belt, bottle, stick, whip ...

_____I've given drugs to others. ____

_____I sold drugs.

_____I've been beaten up (multiple times).

_____I've been given drugs against my knowledge.

_____I've woken up in a different place than where I last remembered.

_____I've been videotaped/photographed for pornography purposes.

_____I've been chained/tied up.

_____I've been choked, tortured.

_____I had foreign objects put inside my body.

_____I put foreign objects inside someone else's body.

_____I've been sexually/physically abused during a religious/ satanic ceremony.

_____I've seen someone being killed.

_____Other: _____.

_____Other: _____.

You might like to know that most survivors check most of the items from the list. They also share, however, that they wish they could block it all out of their memory because it's too painful. The truth is ...

You've been used, abused, manipulated, beaten, violated and more.

You've made poor choices, done some terrible things and have regrets.

But, did you know that most people don't consider you a criminal but someone who was victimized?

You have been controlled and coerced, forced and manipulated. You've been loved and you've been used. Your situation is familiar and helps you to feel like you belong, but you also feel hate and disgust. You're confused.

Survivor Sharing

(Thoughts shared in this section come from people who have been through tough, terrible, traumatic things.)

- *For many nights I lay awake listening to his breathing as I contemplated leaving. Could I? Should I? I was tired of this life and of how it made me feel. I'd tried to escape once before and got caught. He beat me so bad I had to go to the hospital emergency room for stitches. He yelled, "You don't leave till I say so – you're mine, I own you!" I was so scared that I didn't try again for a while, and besides, he kept a closer watch on me after that. But slowly, as the decision to leave grew, I planned my escape once again. This time, I was able to sneak out while he was sleeping. When I finally got out I told myself, "No one owns me! I'm not a piece of property!"*

  Anonymous

- *The night before I got arrested, I got on my knees in the hotel room and cried out to God to help me. Once I was in handcuffs, I was relieved and knew God heard my cry and that I was never going back.*

  Anonymous

- *My only choices at that time were 1. stick around and be killed 2.*

kill myself or 3. at least make an attempt to get out and live.

9to20 Blog, February, 2012

- *Something in me clicked. As the trick stood naked in front of me in the smelly hotel room and handed me the money, I decided I'd had enough! I took the money, threw it at his feet on the floor and walked out. I felt free for the first time in a long time. When my pimp realized I'd left and he couldn't control me anymore, someone told me that he said, "That bitch was getting too old anyway."*

Anonymous

- *I'm glad I left The Life when I think about ...*

  - *The struggles*
  - *The cruelty of The Life*
  - *Getting my kids back*

  - *My safety*
  - *The horrible things that happened to me*

- *Even in my own personal story, the "fear of the unknown" was hugely powerful. At least I could somewhat expect the pain of the old life. If I tried to leave – that was a whole new kind of fear and pain to figure out. How was I to know if it was going to be better or worse? Thankfully, I took that chance one day, but it was a great, GREAT leap. Maybe one day others will understand the worth in this leap of faith as well.*

9to20 Blog, June 10, 2012

Your Story

→ What lies have you believed?

a. *No one can or will help me.*

b. *It's all my fault, I chose this.*

c. *I'm not worth saving.*

For me, I believed that _____.

Thoughts, Feelings, Reflections and/or Doodles

CHAPTER 6

Packed Bags

The desire to leave needs to be greater than the desire to stay.

Elisa's Story

I started to become fairly regular in the emergency room. The nurses had begun to remember me. They remembered my name at least.

I don't remember how I got to the hospital this time. I don't even remember most of what AJ did to me. I just remember waiting in the emergency room for what seemed like a century as everybody else was taken in to be treated.

Finally, a nurse named Sara came and said it was my turn. I tried to stand up to follow her, but a pain shot down my back and I fell back into my seat after only standing up a few inches. The nurse didn't say anything, just walked away and came back a few moments later with a wheelchair.

I was able to limply lift my body into the chair.

"What would you rate your pain level as on a scale from one to ten, ten being absolutely unbearable?"

I thought about it a moment. "Which pain?" I asked.

Sara paused as she took in my bruised face, torn jeans, and hunched back. "Overall."

I thought about it for a moment. "Seven." She nodded and continued to wheel me through the long hallway and into a larger space where I could see patients peeking out from behind drawn white curtains.

I was lying in bed, resting behind closed white curtains when Sara pulled back the white material and let two strange ladies into the small space enclosed behind the curtains. I stared at the two ladies and they stared back for a few moments, none of us knowing what to say.

Finally, Sara spoke up. "Elisa, I've told these women what I think is going on with you. They are social workers and would be able to help you if you let them."

My chest tightened and my heart started pounding louder, faster.

"Hi, Elisa," the younger of the two women said. "I'm Amelia and this is Nancy." She motioned to the older lady who smiled down at me.

Amelia's name struck my heart. A memory of Emelia when she was four years old came to mind. She had asked if I was OK after I had fallen down and scraped my knee. I remembered her big, worried eyes and how, even though she was so young, she had tried to take care of me.

"Hi," I choked out.

"Hi, darling," the older woman, Nancy, said. Her eyes were glowing down at me.

"Elisa," Amelia started, "can you tell us what happened?"

I stared at both of them for a few long moments. "My boyfriend, he ..." I couldn't finish. I didn't think I could tell these two women.

Amelia and Nancy just nodded at me.

"The nurse said this is your fourth time in here over the past few months."

I nodded again, hot tears starting to sting my eyes and slide down my cheeks.

Amelia reached for my hand. She enclosed it in hers and gave a squeeze that I'm sure she thought was reassuring.

"Elisa, we know several shelters for women such as yourself. You will be safe there. We would love if we could help you transition into one of them. This can't go on. We are told your injuries are getting worse and worse every time."

Worse and worse every time. It was true, wasn't it? This beating had been pretty awful; my back and head ached, not to mention between my legs.

If this had happened two months ago, would I have put up with it? Worse and worse every time. What would happen next time?

I started to cry. My body started to shake as sobs wracked my body. The sobbing agitated my back, and I felt pain sharp around my middle. My breathing hitched at the pain and I had trouble getting a steady flow of air back. I started to hyperventilate.

The same nurse who brought the two social workers oversaw me struggling to breathe and came over to calm me down.

She asked the two ladies to step away for a moment.

Amelia's eyes looked so sad as they met mine. "We'll be back tomorrow. Think about what we talked about," she said, as they slowly backed away and headed upstairs, I could only assume to see another struggling girl.

I wasn't supposed to leave the next morning, but I insisted. I took whatever drugs I could find and figured if I got high enough on my usual drugs, then I wouldn't be able to feel the pain as much. I was feeling a little bit better.

I couldn't face those women again. I left before they could come back.

I took a bus home. When I arrived at the house, some of the other girls just looked at me and nodded their heads. Veronica pretended to ignore me, but she brought me a glass of water, which is more than she had ever done for me before in her entire life. Probably more than she'd ever done for anyone in her entire life.

I sat down on my bed and stared at my feet, thinking. I had thought a lot on the bus as well, and I mostly had a plan formed in my mind.

I went to my dresser and pulled out my old ballerina jewelry box from when I was young. It had one of those flimsy keys to open it, which I kept on my keychain.

I looked around and made sure no one was watching before quickly unlocking the box and sitting on the bed. Stashed inside, I had been putting away some money, fearful that if I got caught I would get another beating.

I picked up the bills and counted them, moving them from my left hand to my right as the numbers went through my head. Four hundred and twenty-one dollars. Will that be enough? I don't know, but it's a start.

In those moments when I would quickly open this box and stash money inside, I wondered why I did it. It had been a subconscious need – hide a couple of dollars away. Save them for later. And it's not that I hadn't wanted to take the money out plenty of times when I was coming down and missing a high. Most of the time I was too high to even remember that this money stash existed.

But in those other moments, when my fingers gripped the key and my eyes sought the jewelry box's place in the dresser drawer, and I would almost – almost – open it and take out the money, something always stopped me. It was a sense of purpose that the money seemed to have – as if it had some higher power and would not stoop so low as to be used for drugs or even food.

But now, the money sang to me in a different way. No longer was it calling "Not yet, not yet," but now, instead, it was saying "Yes, now, get out."

I stared down at the money for a few moments while I made a decision. My two options forward seemed to play tug of war in my head.

Should I leave right now in this moment, take the money and leave?

Or should I hide this away and continue to save up? I would surely need more money than this to be on my own.

I stared down at the cash and my mind seemed to change with every beat of my heart.

Go now.

Wait.

Run.

You need more.

You can do it.

You need to wait.

I sighed. Just then, I heard the front door swing open in a confident way that always meant AJ was here. My heart jumped into a sprint and I quickly locked the box, jumped up, and shoved it in my dresser drawer. I closed the drawer and sat back down on my bed. I stared at the floor and tried to calm myself to the point where my chest would stop heaving.

By the time the bedroom door creaked open, I was staring out the window and taking deep breaths.

I couldn't look at him.

"Elisa." AJ's voice was so soft, barely a whisper. It carried a measure of tenderness that I hadn't heard for a long time.

I felt as if my heart was caving in on itself.

"Elisa," he whispered again. I tried not to look up, but it was as if there was some type of magnetic force that was pulling my eyes up to meet his.

His face was very still. He looked like he didn't know what to say. This struck my heart again. AJ always knew what to say.

"Elisa," he said my name a third time, this time staring into my eyes – which felt like my soul.

Two things seemed to play in my mind simultaneously as I looked at him. One was all the moments – the hugs, the looks, his hand in mine– that made me feel safe. The other was its contradiction – all the times he had made me feel so, so small. All the times where I had come away with bruises and tears.

These two scenes played one after the other, on two different screens in my mind, and they seemed to be fighting over which screen was first – which lens I was going to choose to see AJ through. The man who loved me and saved me or the AJ who hurt me and beat me?

Somehow, I think AJ knew what was running through my head in those few moments. He stood there, waiting.

"AJ," I started, but I was still torn between the two AJs. I didn't know how to start, didn't know what to say.

AJ slowly walked across the room, still holding my eyes as he did. Again, it was the most unsure he had ever seemed. Where was his confidence? His certainty? His pride?

"May I sit?" he asked. I nodded my head slowly.

He sat down and stared at me for a few moments. Then he slowly pulled me to his chest and held me. My heart started beating faster– it felt like a herd of horses trying to make wind inside of my chest. Tears began to roll down my cheeks and AJ pulled me closer.

I kept crying. "It's OK, Elisa, it's OK. It's going to be alright." He stroked my wild hair, running his fingers down through the tangles. "You will be alright." Certainty began to return to his voice.

I was going to be alright.

AJ's voice was so smooth and so certain as he sat with me, I felt my heart start to calm and my body begin to relax into his embrace.

"Take a deep breath," he whispered into my ear.

I breathed in. My heart pounded.

I breathed out. My heart pounded.

I need to leave. I've been here before.

"Pack a bag," AJ said, slowly standing up. "You're going to stay with me tonight." *I need to get out of here.* He looked down at me and then pulled me up off the bed into his arms. "I'm going to make sure you're alright."

I took another deep breath, nodded my head, and packed what I needed to leave ... him. (To be continued ...)

_____

Reflections

After a lot of struggles, Elisa has made the decision to leave. Although we can see the roadblocks that are in her life, we can also see that she wants to be out on her own and out of the chaos. We can imagine her saying, "I am not sure what will happen, but I know I don't want to keep living this way any longer." Maybe you have had thoughts like these or others from similar situations at one point in your life:

1. *I'm going to "save up" (stash some cash - if it's safe - and/or gradually take clothes to a friend's place).*

2. *I'll just make a run for it when I get a chance or I'll make a carefully laid plan ahead of time.*

3. *I'm going to make a change and I believe I can be brave enough to do it.*

4. *I'll call the hotline to talk to someone about my options.*

5. *I want to be out on my own, out of this chaotic life.*

6. *It's about time!*

These thoughts are not bad, instead these thoughts sound like a person who is a survivor - someone who has lived through many hard, painful, and violent things - like you.

If you are still trapped, you might be wondering, *Why have I waited so long? Why didn't I decide to leave sooner? Who do I tell or where do I go for help? Where am I going to stay? What can I learn from my past attempts and mistakes?* You are not alone. We believe that you too can leave.

Oftentimes, the controlling people in our lives try to make us feel like we have made the choice to be with them, to do what they ask and to stay. The reality is, did you really have a choice? Many who have left these relationships later say they now realize they didn't really have a choice – whether for fear of retaliation, harm, survival, not having anywhere to go for help, or other reasons. The following statements are designed to help you see where your daily life choices have been taken from you, which could help you decide what you should do.

Life Choices? Do I really have a choice?

Be brutally honest as you circle YES or NO for the following statements.

Yes No 1. I didn't have to have sex with my boyfriend if I didn't feel like it.

Yes No 2. My boyfriend and I decided together where we would live.

Yes No 3. I usually got to wear what I wanted to wear and not what I was told to wear.

Yes No 4. I got to choose what kind of food I ate most of the time.

Yes No 5. If I didn't want to work, I didn't have to.

Yes No 6. I was able to choose how I wanted to spend the money I made.

Yes No 7. I could leave anytime I wanted to, without fear of what would happen.

Yes No 8. I didn't have to work if I felt sick.

Yes No 9. We decided together about when and where I would work.

Yes No 10. If I didn't have a good feeling, I could refuse a buyer.

Yes No 11. Each night I worked, I could stop when I was tired or after a bad buyer.

Yes No 12. I got to have a say in decisions and what we did.

Yes No 13. I made most of my own choices and decisions about my life and my future.

Yes No 14. I got to choose whether or not to have a baby or an abortion.

Yes No 15. My feelings, wishes and desires were listened to and not ignored.

Yes No 16. Other: _____

Yes No 17. Other: _____

Yes No 18. Other: _____

by BC Johnson, 2011

Did you answer *No* to any or most of the statements? If so, now is the time to think seriously about leaving.

> Staying or Leaving?
> I want to stay.
> We're going to be together forever.
> Why would I leave?
>
> I want to stay.
> Even though he's sometimes violent.
> Why would I leave?
>
> I want to stay – most of the time.
> Even though I'm scared and hate my life.
> Why would I leave?
>
> I'm not sure I want to stay.
> But life's hard and no one's perfect
> What would I do and where would I go IF I left?
>
> I'm not sure I want to stay.
> The hard times are more frequent than the good times.
> Maybe I should leave.
>
> I don't want to stay.
> But I don't think I CAN leave. I feel stuck and trapped.
> I wish I could leave.
>
> I don't want to stay.
> I know life is hard and that the future is filled with
> uncertainties but,
> I am going to leave.
>
> I'm not going to stay.
> I'm going to get out and get on with my life.
> I'm leaving.
>
> I left.

BC Johnson, 2015

Survivor Sharing

(Thoughts shared in this section come from people who have been through tough, terrible, traumatic things.)

- *As a way of coping, I used to say that being in The Life was my choice, that it was exciting and a rush, because that was so much easier than admitting to myself that I was a victim.*

  9 to 20 Blog, November, 2011

- *I called a regular and asked for help to escape my pimp. I am so thankful that he said "Yes" and helped me get out.*

  Anonymous

- *I had to quickly leave with only the clothes on my back, not because I was being impulsive but because I only had a few minutes when he wasn't watching me. It wasn't impulsive because I'd been thinking about it for a long time.*

  Anonymous

- *It wasn't safe to stash money for when I was going to leave. I had to be willing to just go, with nothing.*

  Anonymous

- *I can't pinpoint the moment where I realized escape really was possible. There were many, many circumstances and people together that made my redemption possible. Somehow all the planets aligned and new life started to occur. I knew that if I stayed I'd either be killed or kill myself, so I chose to jump in faith and run.*

  9to20 Blog, October, 2011

- *"Why didn't you run?" This is easily the No. 1 question I'm asked when people hear about my story. Wanting to leave is much, much different though than knowing how to leave.*

  9to20 Blog, October 26, 2011

Your Story

So, you've decided to leave. You still have fears and doubts, but you realize that you can't go on like this. Your head and heart agree most of the time that it's best to get out.

Quick – write down all the reasons you are leaving. If you're afraid of the list being seen, write it in your own made-up code language that only you will understand.

But, WRITE IT DOWN somewhere, somehow, now!

That list will help keep you on the path to freedom. When you doubt the decision to leave, when you're missing him or someone else, when you feel uncomfortable, when you're confused, go back and read the list.

Memorize it!

As you make your list, maybe it will be helpful to read what others have said:

What I Hated about being in The Life

- *I hated being completely oppressed*
- *Being beaten constantly*
- *I felt "less than"*
- *My pimp would let his friends do horrible things to me*
- *Being told what to do, having no freedom*
- *Moving around a lot*
- *Having to beat or hurt others*
- *The shame and guilt I constantly felt*
- *Disgusting johns and dirty hotels*
- *The constant revolving door of jail*
- *Feeling like "shit," always feeling dirty*
- *The continual lies*
- *Having to give up all the money I made*
- *The deception and betrayal*
- *Having to lie*
- *Doing porn*
- *Having to recruit others*
- *Being "raped" over and over*
- *Not knowing who I am anymore/not recognizing myself*

My List

Thoughts, Feelings, Reflections and/or Doodles

CHAPTER 7

The Shelter

I think Shakespeare wrote, "Parting is such sweet sorrow." In this case, it isn't!

Elisa's Story

After AJ fell asleep, I wondered, *Is this where I belong?* When that thought ran through my head, my heart recognized that it was a lie. This was not where I belonged. I pushed myself up onto my elbows and looked down at AJ as he was sleeping half a foot from me. He looked peaceful in his sleep. *Did I ever look that peaceful?*

As I started walking across the room, my heart fluttered. I let out a breath as I turned around and saw AJ still sleeping. I then proceeded to grab my clothes, get dressed, and get my bag as quietly as possible. Looking at AJ, he did not stir. Determination filled my being. Tiptoeing quickly to the front door, I unpacked my comfy shoes, put them on, and left.

Now what? What do I do now?

The first thing that went through my mind was to take a bus for about thirty minutes to a part of the city I've rarely worked. I found the first motel I could and paid thirty-five precious dollars for a room.

The room was a piece of trash, but I still found myself overwhelmed with relief when I closed the door and locked it behind me. I stood there, back against the door, observing the tiny and disgusting room, and breathed an enormous sigh.

I stayed there that night. I just lay in the bed and stared at the ceiling, falling in and out of sleep. I was still in so much pain, especially in my lower back, and I let the pain fade away into a haze of drugs and sleep.

When I woke, the voice in my head was "How can I help you?" It was then that I remembered the lady who had given me the card months ago. I had thrown the card away, but I had the numbers swimming around in my mind.

I called again and this time, I answered her question.

Getting to the shelter was a blur. I think I remember a lady answering the phone. I can't remember what she said, but it must have been about where I was staying, because somehow, the next thing that was happening was I was being picked up by a woman with curly, silvery hair who looked like she fell out of a gardening magazine. She had on work clothes, dirty boots, and an annoyingly friendly smile.

"Elisa?" she inquired with a questioning eyebrow as I opened the door.

I nodded, wiping my eyes. Her face was still a little bit fuzzy.

She smiled. "I'm Anna." She held out her hand. "We talked on the phone."

I stared down at her hand for a moment before I realized I was supposed to shake it.

Anna smiled at me again after I shook her hand. "Do you need help bringing anything out to the van?" I looked down at my small bag that I had somehow already packed and shook my head.

"Just this," I said, my voice sounding a bit husky.

Anna nodded. "Well then, follow me." She started walking to the van. I glanced one last time at the safety of the room behind me. My heart, which had been chugging along, began to beat faster.

I hesitated while taking my first step out the door. However, once I rapidly took that first step and looked up to see Anna waiting for me by the van, my confidence grew. It felt right.

I carried my bag to the van and set it by my feet in the front passenger seat.

"You ready?" I looked up and saw Anna waiting for my response.

I nodded. She still looked at me though, as if my nod wasn't enough.

"Yes," I said. "I'm ready."

And that's the thing – I was ready.

It was my third day at the temporary emergency women's shelter. It was my first day of true coherence though. I woke up feeling a strange sort of clarity. The ceiling suddenly became interesting, the details coming into focus. I stared at the ceiling for as long as I could before I knew that I had to get up.

I had been reminded several times that today there was an information session I was required to go to if I was going to continue staying at the shelter.

I pushed myself off the bed and stood for a few minutes as my feet grew accustomed to the cold, wood floor. There were two other beds in the small room, but both the other ladies seemed to have left already.

I looked at the clock above the door and realized I had limited time before I would have to be downstairs. Even though I was in a hurry, I took my time as I walked to the bathroom. I splashed cold water onto my face and then observed my reflection as the clear drops ran down my face and into the sink.

I looked slightly less hollow. I realized in that moment that is what I had become – hollow. I had turned into a fragile, bruised shell whose eyes had turned dark and whose cheeks curved in instead of out. But my eyes looked slightly lighter today. There was even a hint of pink in my cheeks. Even though my body ached, and my stomach was in one large knot, I looked much better on the outside.

I drummed my fingers on the counter. I really needed a fix. I wasn't allowed though. Which I guess I understood. But I really, really needed a fix.

But you're doing better already without it. Look at yourself.

I looked at myself one more time before leaving the bathroom. I stared at my reflection and wondered if my face was the face a younger sister could be proud of.

What would Emmy think?

Before I could answer, I swung the door open and walked through it, heading downstairs to the required meeting. (To be continued ...)

Reflections

Elisa left. It was really hard for her and incredibly challenging. She made it, though, and has spent several days in a place where she was safe – very different than what she experienced with AJ. They not only let her sleep, but they have started to help her figure out her next steps. You might be thinking that you are so glad she left and that it sounds scary, but definitely not as scary as some of the stuff you've had to put up within your traumatic situations. You might also be thinking, Just like Elisa, I did it! I was brave! I made a change – *for the better too!*

Despite your first initial reaction, you might also be wondering, Did I make the right decision? Why didn't I leave sooner?! What is going to happen to me now? What if he finds me? Should I still take on a few regulars – you know, the ones who are kind?

Just like Elisa, you might be quickly wondering what to do, where you will live, and what your first step will be. Your journey will be different than that of *Pretty Woman* or Disney movies with their magical rescues. You will not find freedom in an instant, rather you are on a journey of growth and recovery that takes a lot of hard work. But we believe that you can do it!

One of the first steps that you will need to take is to acknowledge the negative things you have gained from your experiences. Some of the survivors that we know who've "been there and done that" talk about the fact that being in The Life has given them a police record, addictions, STIs, physical injuries, infertility, scars from being beaten, and the reality that verbal abuse can leave an imprint that no one else can see.

We have to be honest with ourselves about the negative things that happened. This lets us see clearly what we have lost and what good things were taken away. Losses are hard and overwhelming, yet many of the things you have lost can be regained with determination and guts – which you already have.

My Losses *(what others have shared)*

- *Being able to trust other people*
- *Being heard and having my opinions and my feelings valued*
- *My identity (my name and an address/location)*
- *A sense of security, safety and stability*
- *Freedom to choose what, when and how I will use my body*
- *Celebrating special holidays and not having to work*
- *Missing family events (birthdays, funerals ...)*
- *Healthy perspective on relationships and sex*
- *Options, choices – the freedom to choose and do and say what I want, when I want*
- *Getting to have a pet*
- *Physical and mental health*
- *Many of my future hopes & dreams*
- *Being able to feel feelings (instead of shutting down or going numb)*
- *Real friends beyond my survivor siblings (wifeys)*

- *Understanding what "normal" is*
- *Feeling worthy or of value, my dignity*
- *Self-confidence, self-esteem and self-respect*
- *Joy and true happiness*
- *Motivation and/or energy to do things other than be in The Life*
- *Naivete, innocence and virginity*
- *Faith in God*
- *My moral compass – knowing what's right and wrong*
- *Going to school and getting an education*
- *Having rights (basic human civil rights) and being treated with respect*
- *Feeling truly accepted for who I am (not just for what I do)*
- *Other:* _____.

Looking at everything that we have lost can leave us feeling mad and sad. It makes me infuriated when I think about everything that my traffickers took from me, leaving me with heavy burdens because of their sick decisions. It is normal to feel mad that you've lost so much and sad because you may think you've lost these things forever. Anger is not a bad emotion – keep it around to help when you're wavering on your decision to stay out. And remember, many of your losses can be regained, mine were.

_____

Survivor Sharing

(Thoughts shared in this section come from people who have been through tough, terrible, traumatic things.)

I don't miss ...	I'm glad I didn't ...
Having sex with nasty guys	Die out there
The chaos	Get killed
Getting beat up	Have to go to prison
The lies	Lose my mind
Being degraded	Run into a serial killer
Worrying about my next fix	Stay
Feeling dirty	

More Thoughts

Change can be hard, and, change can be painful, even when it's the best thing to do.

Too often we get comfortable and settle for people who are unhealthy and places that are dangerous. Rather than change, we accept the situation. We continue because it's familiar, because it's all we know or because we don't know what to do, where to go or because we don't feel we deserve anything better than this.

Even though it can be hard, change is often the right thing to do. We need to move on. We need to make a change. WE need to break free, to break away.

Even positive, desired changes can be challenging as we adjust to new situations, people or possibilities. You've already shown your bravery and taken a step toward change by even reading this book.

Change is also very emotionally hard, especially when we focus on the good memories and neglect the bad ones. We know in our head that leaving is the right thing to do but our heart is confused, lonely, doubting, and shame-filled. This is to be expected – to have doubts and uncertainties.

When we make a change, we must remind ourselves why we decided to leave in the first place. Whether we're leaving a destructive relationship, quitting an old habit, exiting a bad situation or whatever it may be, we must remember why we made the decision we did. It will give us the strength to beat the temptation to go back.

Change brings uncertainties.

When breaking free, you don't always know where you're going or what you're going to do. You just know that you must make a change.

Hope and help are available. Some places to call and organizations that want to help are listed in the back of the book under Resources.

_____

Your Story

→ Add to your "Why I left list" from the end of the last chapter and read it aloud.

→ What did The Life steal from you?

→ What are some ways that you can reclaim what you have lost?

→ Describe several ways that you can use anger for good?

Thoughts, Feelings, Reflections and/or Doodles

CHAPTER 8

The Hotel

To live by choice, not by chance
To make changes, not excuses
To be motivated, not manipulated
To be useful, not used
To try again, even in defeat
I choose self-esteem, not self-pity
I choose to listen to the positive inner voice
Not the internalized lies of others
– Unknown, adapted

Elisa's Story

I fought hard to fall asleep that night, but somehow the shores of sleep did not welcome me.

I kept on seeing AJ's face in my mind. AJ. My boyfriend.

No. My pimp.

I gagged every time that thought ran through my head.

My pimp.

I was angry. I was so #$@&%*! mad.

I couldn't sleep because I was lying in bed with my heart on fire. It was pounding faster and faster, burning bigger and bigger. I kept on changing position in bed, trying to find one that would make me less angry. Or angrier. I don't know.

My hands were clenched by my sides. I would bring them up to my chest and hold them together tight.

I hadn't felt this way since the first few nights Bill came into my room all those years ago. After he left each time I would spend the rest of the night trying to contain all the awful feelings pouring out of me. I would hold my knees to my chest, knowing that if I let the feelings out, they would drift into the world and everyone would know my shame.

After a while I realized that I certainly was not going to get any amount of sleep like this.

I looked around the room to make sure the other women were asleep. I slid down from my bunk and reached into my pack. I reached into the front pocket and unzipped the smaller, secretive pocket within that one.

My hands enclosed around a small ziplock bag. My body sank in a sigh of relief as my fingers pulled the bag out. I looked around the room one more time before tiptoeing to the restroom.

I didn't look in the mirror this time. I wasn't able to.

I took a few pills and sat on the floor for a few moments and just breathed as I waited for the drugs to hit my system.

The next four days were a bit of a blur.

All I know is that any time I began to sober up, I began to feel too much.

Too much anger. Too much despair. Too much worthlessness.

And yet, Anna and the others who worked there told me that I wasn't worthless. They treated me with kindness, care, and respect. Something I hadn't experienced since I was a little girl.

The end of the week came too soon. The end of the week meant it was the end of my time in the shelter.

"Elisa." Anna said my name. It felt good to hear my real name, instead of my street name. "Elisa, are you listening?"

"We don't have any openings currently in our long-term transition housing, but I put you at the top of our waiting list. And I suggest you apply right away for short-term housing with Freedom Home so you have somewhere to stay until a spot opens up for you on our end."

I nodded my head, showing my understanding.

"I stopped by Freedom Home this morning and picked up an application for you. You should fill it out right now and I'll take it over after. Tonight is your last night here, so I'll try and make sure Freedom Home can take you right away."

Anna handed me the application and I reached for it. The few pages stapled together somehow seemed like overwhelming weights in my hands.

"Elisa." I looked up at her as she said my name. "You're doing well. Let's make sure this continues." Anna's face showed loving concern as she said this.

Was I doing better, though? I didn't necessarily feel that way. I felt numb, both physically and emotionally.

"Thank you," I responded, trying to bring meaning to it.

Anna nodded again while I sat down with the application and a pen.

I was trying to read the words on the page but, however the words were strung together, I was unable to find any meaning in them. *What were they asking me?*

I stared at the pages a few more minutes, while multiple thoughts ran through my head. Did I even want to go to another home? What good would that do me?

No, I could do this on my own.

I had always relied on other people, and look where that got me. The boyfriend who saved me had become my pimp.

No. I was going to do this on my own.

———

I was in the motel by myself for about three days before I dared to leave it behind me. I should have been searching for food to sustain me, but instead, what finally pulled me out of the appalling room was my need for more drugs. The pills from the hospital and drugs from AJ were gone. I knew there were some people I could call, but I was too afraid. Word would probably get back to AJ.

Instead, I did the next best thing – I walked down the streets surrounding my motel and took in the people around me. I observed them as I passed, searching for the signs I knew all too well.

I walked around a few times before I was sure who I wanted to approach. He was tall and bone skinny, with light, sandy-brown hair. His eyes were too close together and they darted around too quickly, looking suspiciously at the world around him.

I approached him, trying to look nonchalant. I had never had to do this outside before, and with strangers. The drugs that revolved around our house were never passed between strangers, but between people who relied on each other for things the other could offer – money, sex, favors.

I walked up to Beady Eye. His eyebrows raised in a skeptical look and his eyes moved up and down my body.

"Hey there, baby." He smiled at me, revealing pointed, yellow teeth.

I nodded at him. "I'm looking for someone to hook me up," I said quietly, not sure whether to look in his eyes or the ground as I said it. I ended up just staring at his rotting teeth. Rules AJ had taught me circulated in my head.

His lips stretched even wider after my words reached his ears.

"Oh, how interesting," he said with his slimy-looking mouth. "I happen to be looking for a hook-up as well." His eyes roamed once again up and down my body and his smile somehow grew even bigger.

I stared at him for a moment. He nodded his head back to an alleyway behind him. He licked his lips.

My heart was pounding in my chest. No. I was supposed to be done with that life. I wanted so badly to turn away, but I looked down at my hand, which was shaking. I needed a high.

I looked at Yellow Teeth. "Let me see your product first."

He laughed. "No, baby. Payment comes first." His eyes once again roamed down my body.

I breathed a heavy sigh.

What was one more? My body wouldn't know the difference, and I was already worthless.

I nodded my head and walked past him into the alley behind. I walked about fifteen feet in, to where it was mostly dark.

I didn't need to turn around to know he had followed me. I had heard his footsteps, heavy behind me, and now I felt his breath close to my ear.

"Turn around and face the wall," he said. I did as I was told, my face staring at the crumbling red brick.

I had barely stood still before I felt his hands reach around and quickly unbutton and unzip my jeans. A moment later, they were yanked down to my ankles.

I let out a short breath and placed my palms on the wall in front of me.

Remember, I told myself, he has the drugs you need.

It was over pretty quickly – quicker than most. He let out a grunt and pulled out. His pants were soon back on.

"You can pull yours back on, too," he said.

I let down my arms from the wall and used them to pull up my underwear and jeans. Once they were secure, I turned around. He was rummaging in his jacket pocket and soon pulled out a tiny, clear bag with white powder in it. My heart started to beat faster.

The man noticed my reaction and his teeth pulled out again to show his slimy, yellow smile.

"It's all yours," he said, handing it to me. "You know where to come if you need any more." He gave one last knowing smile before dropping the bag in my hand and walking back down the alley.

I stared at the bag in my hand, but in my mind, I still saw his slimy smile.

I had been working out of the motel for a few weeks. Yellow Teeth had a few friends he sent my way, and I picked up a few on the street corners around the motel.

It hadn't been my intention to start sleeping around again, but my jewelry box money stash was soon emptied and I needed somewhere to stay. I also always seemed to need more drugs. I think I saw Yellow Teeth more than I saw anyone else, but his product was good and his price never seemed to increase.

It was probably the best deal I could have hoped for.

While I had people in and out of my motel room each night, I still felt a profound sense of loneliness, along with intense feelings of anger, self-hatred, and depression.

I told myself what I was doing wasn't any different from before, but somehow, I felt even cheaper than I had with AJ's clients. AJ had known my name. He had touched me tenderly. His clients knew that there were rules in place – things you could and could not do with his girls.

The men I was entertaining knew no such thing, and some nights I really struggled to draw the line. I think the problem was I myself didn't know where the line was, so how could I show it to someone else?

There were some mornings where I would wake up and feel safe, and oftentimes on those mornings I would reach out to try and find AJ – but of course he wasn't there.

I realized at these times that all the special moments in my life where I had felt the absolute safest had happened in AJ's apartment, with him there.

That realization made it hard to hate him. I knew he had used me, but did that mean he hadn't loved me? I had always felt like he treated me differently than the other girls. Maybe I was different. (To be continued ...)

Reflections

This chapter begins with Elisa having to make major decisions about her future. Although some staff members wanted to help her do the paperwork for a housing program, it was overwhelming and scary for Elisa. In the past she had to manage everything on her own: protecting Emmy, keeping secrets, and dealing with Bill. Since she had no help all those years, it makes sense that she thinks she can handle the process of figuring out housing on her own too. Tangled into her past experiences and feelings of loneliness and self-hate, Elisa was also believing the lies, *I need to do it myself. No one can really help me. I cannot trust anyone. And I am beyond help.* Maybe you have experienced some of these negative beliefs, as well as felt some of these same enticing thoughts and luring feelings.

Yet, the reality is that although there are many unsafe people in this world, there are also many safe people. We know that is hard to believe, especially if you've never experienced it. There are people who want to help protect you, people who want to help you embrace hope, people who genuinely care, not because they want to get something from you – rather because they want to empower you to be free and to embrace your dreams. When these and other negative beliefs come, we must learn to fight them. So how do you that?

Our minds are super amazing. We can take the lies we believe and replace them with truth. For instance, if we believe that no one cares, through experiencing someone who does care we can begin to rewrite the lies with the truth that, "There are some safe people who care very much about us, our pain, and our needs." I experienced this when, after having several really awful experiences with medical providers, I ended up having a very positive one. It showed me that some medical providers can be helpful, kind, and caring. Now whenever I go to the doctor, I do a reality check and remind myself that not all doctors are bad. Rather, some doctors are genuinely sensitive and helpful.

The first step to fighting the lies we believe is to recognize them. With each lie you believe, make a truth statement (like the following examples). Repeat the truth back to yourself out loud – over and over again. Some people like to make cards with the truth and put them on mirrors or other places frequently seen. Others have set a timer on their phone and recite their truth statements at a certain time each day.

The following list of lies was compiled from talking to many survivors of prostitution. Choose the lies you most tell yourself. We have added examples of truth that we hope can help. You probably won't believe these truth statements at first but keep reading them – over and over again. Repetition can help you get rid of the lies and begin to believe the truth.

Lies and Truths about Sexual Exploitation

Some of the many LIES we believe	Some TRUTH statement examples
No one can really help me.	The right people can help me if they are safe.
I'm worthless.	I am not worthless.
I'm a nobody.	I am human.
I'm a slut (ho, bitch, whore).	Sex does not define me.
I don't deserve anything good to happen to me.	I deserve good things to happen to me.
I can't trust anyone.	Some people are trustworthy.
I am to blame. It's all my fault.	It is not my fault.
No one will help or can help.	There are safe people in the world who can help.
No one cares.	Safe people do care.
I can't do anything right.	I can do some things right. I am trustworthy.
I chose this life.	I did not choose this life. It was chosen for me.
I can't make any good decisions.	I can make good decisions. I am trustworthy.
I'll never change.	Others have changed. I can change.

Some of the many LIES we believe	Some TRUTH statement examples
Life won't or can't get any better.	Life can get better.
My exploiter really does love me.	My exploiter wanted me to think that it was love.
My feelings don't matter.	My feelings are important.
Good things won't happen to me.	Good things are in my future.
I should have tried harder.	I am strong and tried very hard. It's not my fault.
I am a bad person.	I am not a bad person.
I should have known better.	I could not have expected what happened.
I must not let things bother me.	It's OK to feel pain.
I must hide or ignore my feelings.	My feelings are important. I am important.
I'll never be good for anything.	I can learn a new skill.
All I'm good at/for is sex.	Sex does not need to define me.
I've got to take care of others.	I need to take care of myself.
I can't trust myself.	I can learn to trust myself.
I am worthless.	I am worthy.
I'm so stupid.	I survived because I am intelligent.
People will always use and abuse me, even those who say they love or care about me.	There are safe people in the world who are very different than my abusers.
I've got to be tough and not let things bother me.	Crying and feeling emotions are not weakness.
Love hurts.	Real love is kind, respectful, and compassionate.
This is what I deserve.	I deserve kindness and respect.
It's helpless (the situation).	The situation is not helpless.
I'm helpless.	I am not helpless.
I'm hopeless.	I am not hopeless.
This is as good as it gets.	There is so much more to life than this.

Sometimes when we replace lies with truth, we might feel a lot of overwhelming emotions. If you have gotten used to numbing your emotions, it might be challenging to identify, feel and express them, but it is possible. Don't give up. Adjusting to any new situation can be challenging, but adjusting to being out of The Life is extra hard because you've been emotionally and mentally manipulated, physically and sexually abused. Knowing what triggers you (what makes you upset, confused or scared) can help you to calm down.

For example, if you are angry and depressed, or you feel powerless, out of control, and not respected, you might need to show yourself kindness, compassion, and self-love. Several ways you can do that is by listening to your favorite music, engaging in a spiritual practice that brings comfort, talking with friends, focusing on your determination and perseverance, drawing or painting, writing, reading, spending time with a pet, hitting a pillow, taking a long shower or bath, dancing, or giving yourself permission to cry. You can also try these coping skills, important for everyone:

- Be patient with yourself and give yourself permission to heal

- Make sure you get up and do something (walk, exercise, yoga ...)

- Eat healthy food (not junk food)

- Do things with safe people – fight the desire to isolate

- Get adequate sleep (don't stay up all day and night)

- Get involved in a support group or program

Survivor Sharing

(Thoughts shared in this section come from people who have been through tough, terrible, traumatic things.)

- *So much of what I was taught growing up was to stuff emotions, to not feel. I couldn't feel if I wanted to survive, I just couldn't. The emotion would have killed me back then. So it was good at that time, for me to go numb. It was necessary. It's now far less necessary*

*and I understand that to truly be healthy I must show emotions ...
this just happens to be an incredibly painful process for me.*

9to20 Blog, August, 2012

▪ *Lies like those have a certain knack for infiltrating the mind at its
weakest moments. I know that these are lies, my mind KNOWS this
... but sometimes it takes my heart a moment to catch up.*

9to20 Blog, July, 2012

Survivors shared these responses to the following statements.
Maybe you've experienced the same things. If so, that is OK.
Please keep reading and please keep moving forward – in a healthy
direction, toward healing and hope.

I am most afraid ...

- *Of going back and failure*

I don't like it when ...

- *I miss The Life*
- *I beat myself up*
- *I listen to the lies in my head*
- *I have nightmares and flashbacks*
- *I get randomly triggered*

I think about going back to The Life when ...

- *I feel lonely*
- *I feel hopeless*
- *My "dirtbag" mindset hits*
- *I want money*
- *I want to numb my feelings*

Sometimes I feel like ...

- *Giving up*
- *Yelling, screaming*
- *Recovery is too hard – but I never give up*

I hate it when:

- *People glamorize The Life*
- *I get stuck feeling bad about myself*
- *I think about going back*

It is important ...
- *To never give up, never surrender*
- *That I'm in recovery*
- *That I don't give a f&#! about him anymore*
- *To let go and let God*
- *To have a relationship with Jesus*

When I think about the future ...
- *I get anxious and scared*
- *I'm hopeful and ready for change*

I need ...
- *Help and support*
- *Help with my issues*
- *Patience*

Missing

Missing what's comfortable
Missing the familiar
Makes me forget the pain

Missing being a "family"
Missing being "loved"
Makes me forget the shame
Missing what feels good
Missing what's known
Makes me believe the lies

It never felt good
It was never a "family"
It was never a "home"
It was never true "love"

I am missing a lie

Your Story

Write down five lies you believe about yourself, others, and the situation you are/were in. Then, write down five truths.

Lies	Truth
1	1
2	2
3	3
4	4
5	5

What are some of the things that help you when your emotions feel overwhelming?

(Examples: listening to music, exercising, reading, taking a shower, being creative, walking, napping ...)

Thoughts, Feelings, Reflections and/or Doodles

CHAPTER 9

Damon AND AJ

I fooled myself into only remembering the good and forgetting the bad.

Elisa's Story

After about a month of living at the motel, I started to notice a man often watching me.

He was incredibly tall and had broad shoulders. He had dark, curly hair that matched the chocolate milk hue of his skin. His eyes were also dark, and they would follow me from across the street whenever I left my motel room. He wouldn't follow me with his feet, but he always followed me with his eyes until I was out of reach. His presence was a dark stain on my days.

After about a week of his unsettling presence outside, I heard a knock on my door one evening. Expecting one of my regular clients, I opened the door to see the dark man standing there.

I stared at him for a moment, not sure what to do or say. He made a move before I had a chance to decide on my own move. He pushed inside, closing the door behind him.

I took a few steps back.

He looked into my eyes with his dark look. "Pack up your things."

I looked around the room at the mess of clothes and trash strewn about. I looked back at him like he was crazy. He couldn't just tell me to leave.

He saw my look and began to pull things off the floor and put them on my bed.

"Pack up your shit, bitch." He yelled at me as he proceeded to throw more things on the bed.

I reached out to grab something out of his hand – *this was my stuff.*

He caught my hand and wrapped his hands around my wrists. He used the hold he had on me to push me backward. I fell onto the bed behind me.

He climbed onto the bed and pushed my arms over my head, his grip still tight on my wrists. My body shook as I tried to break free of his grasp. He had me pinned to the bed.

"Bitch, I don't know who you think you are," His face was inches from mine and his breath was hot against my skin. "But no one is a renegade in my town."

His hands grabbed the bottom of my shirt and pulled it up over my head. I expected to feel his hands, but when I didn't, I finally looked up at him. He was just looking at me, like I was a piece of property.

He nodded his head and pulled my shirt back down. He then looked into my eyes.

"Time to go, bitch." He stepped off the bed and motioned with his hand at all the junk still on the floor.

I quietly stood up and pulled out my bag from under the bed.

"Time to make me my money," he said, with a daring glint in his eyes.

———————

Time flew by.

I reached for the dime bag that I usually kept in my bra, but my hands came back empty. It has to be here somewhere. I reached for my purse and quickly rifled through it.

Come on.

I turned my purse over onto my bed and quickly spread everything out, searching, searching ...

"Ahh!" I yelled and threw my purse down on the dirty ground. I looked over at some of the girls in their beds. Most of them ignored me, but some of them were giving me looks.

I yelled again. "Damn it!"

I sat down on the bed and put my head in my hands. I could feel my heart pounding.

I needed a fix.

"Go into the client room," Mirabella, the girl on the bed to my left, said. "Damon will give you some drugs after you service a few clients."

I looked at Mirabella. She was laying in her bed staring at the ceiling. She went to blink, but her eyes were so tired that they stayed shut a few seconds before opening again.

I stared at the door out to the hallway. At the front of the house was the client room. Damon kept us all back here, strung out on our highs most of the time. But my high was ending and I didn't have any more.

I stared at the door with a sinking feeling in my stomach. I took a deep breath and made my way out the door and down the hall.

Damon demanded so much more than I had ever even known was possible. He was more violent and would regularly rape me. Even AJ's worst days seemed so much easier than what I was going through now.

So, when I got a chance a few weeks later, I decided to run. Right back to AJ.

I missed him and hoped that he had missed me too. Oh, how my heart to experience his tenderness and feel safe again.

I left early one morning and dialed the numbers I knew by heart. AJ didn't even seem surprised to hear from me. I tried to detect any anger in his voice, but instead I heard the tones of relief as he told me to come back home.

"Baby, I missed you so much."

My heart melted and I couldn't wait to see him. For the first time in months, I felt the bubble of hope rise in my stomach.

When I saw AJ, I wanted to collapse into his arms and have him hold me. I was shocked when what I met first was his fist.

AJ beat me, screaming as he did it. He threatened me to never run away again. That night, he kicked me out and told me he wouldn't let me back in without money. The amount he yelled was more than I had ever made in a single night in my life.

I was terrified. How was I going to make that much?

As days and weeks went by, I felt stupid and thought about how hard it was to leave this life behind. But I couldn't leave. I wasn't good for anything else, and I found security in knowing what each day would bring, rather than the uncertainty of the big world called my future.

I regretted having left, but I also regretted coming back. (To be continued ...)

Reflections

We know that Elisa's story might be heavy and overwhelming for you to read, especially if you are thinking about going back or have returned in the past. It is heavy for us, too. Our hearts hurt at the pain Elisa, you, and others have survived and continue to experience.

Many of the survivors who we have worked with have indicated that stress, exhaustion, loneliness and hunger make the thoughts about going back more intense. In this state, it is easy to remember only the good times and not the bad. You might miss the familiar, whether it is hurtful or harmful. We want you to know that there is no shame in thinking these thoughts. Instead, it creates an opportunity where you can make the choice to stay. A choice that belongs to you alone!

After making the decision to stay you might feel regret. Why didn't I leave him sooner? *Why did I hurt others, even though I was told to do so? And, why didn't I see the truth sooner?* Regret is an interesting emotion, one in which we tend to blame ourselves for a bad experience. Here we might feel extreme grief for the consequences of the choices we have made. If you focus on your regret you will stop moving forward. You will stay stuck in your mistakes and misfortunes, forgetting the lessons you've learned and strengths gained.

Regret often keeps people locked up in the past – but keep on going. You need to grieve the losses you have endured and focus on the future and what you want different for your life. Every mistake is an opportunity to do better the next time.

Change is hard and there will be times you will need to tough it out. Yet, you've survived so much and you will get through this too!

I regret leaving.
I regret not leaving sooner.

I regret going back.
I regret getting others into The Life.
I regret hurting others.
I regret not seeing the truth sooner.
I regret staying.
I regret lots of things.

I regret leaving.
I regret not leaving sooner.

Just Because

Just because ...

You miss him, doesn't mean you should go back to be with him.

You miss The Life, doesn't mean you should return.

You miss the good parts, doesn't mean you should forget the many bad parts.

Just because ...

You think you'd be better off just going back to The Life, doesn't mean you should.

You think you'll never fit in anywhere else, doesn't mean you should stop trying.

You think you don't deserve anything good, doesn't mean you don't.

Just because ...

You feel like life won't get better, doesn't mean it won't.

You feel like a nobody, doesn't mean you are.

You feel like giving up trying, doesn't mean you should.

Just because ...

You are overwhelmed now, doesn't mean you will always be.

You are scared now, doesn't mean you will always be afraid.

You don't know what the future holds, doesn't mean you should give up.

Just because ...

You don't like your new life at times, doesn't mean you should give it up.

You learned to distrust people, doesn't mean you should never trust ever again.

You were told no one can love you like he does, doesn't mean it is true.

Just because ...

You are scared, doesn't mean you shouldn't try.

You are confused, doesn't mean you should give up.

You don't know what real love it, doesn't mean you can't experience it, because you can.

You *can* make it through this.

You *are* strong – look at what you've already survived (MUCH harder than this)!

You *do* have value and worth.

Don't give in – don't give up.

But, if you fall, get back up, however long it takes. Keep walking away from The Life and the lies it shouts into your head and heart that you can't change, because you can.

It may be hard but it is possible and so worth it!

Becca C. Johnson, 2011

Survivor Sharing

(Thoughts shared in this section come from people who have been through tough, terrible, traumatic things.)

- *I learned to ignore my emotions, I didn't allow myself to feel, I needed to be numb, it helped me to survive. But now I know that to be truly healthy I must learn to feel and it's OK and important to experience the range of my emotions even though it is an incredibly painful process for me.*

  Anonymous

- *As cheesy as it sounds, you are worth and deserve better. The scars remain but the mind will change.*

  Anonymous

- *You gotta feel it to heal it! It might hurt but that's necessary on the road to recovery from being in The Life.*

  Anonymous

- *Stay strong and positive and desire to want to have a normal, healthy life. You can do it!*

  Anonymous

- *Life is worth living and you don't have to resort to this life full of chaos. You'll never have the freedom or peace you search for. It only gets worse – jails, hospitals and killers are all out there, a life full of darkness that will suffocate and kill you. God is the answer. He will save you. There are people and programs that will and can help you.*

  Anonymous

- *NO ONE deserves it! You deserve SO MUCH MORE!*

  Anonymous

- *At first I was in denial but it didn't take long and I was sorry I'd gone back.*

  Anonymous

I'm Doubting and Hoping

I'm doubting ...
   Myself, my decisions, my ability to make decisions
I'm doubting ...
   If I'm doing the right thing, If anyone can be trusted
I'm doubting ...
   If real love exists, my future, Life itself
I'm doubting!

I'm hoping ...
    that I'll figure this out, that I'll do the right thing
I'm hoping ...
    I'll find people to help me, find a place to stay and get
    my life back.
I'm hoping ...
    I'll get out, stay out and stay strong.
I'm hoping!

Your Story

→ What emotions come up when you hear people talking about returning to The Life?

→ At the end of Elisa's story in this chapter, we read "I regretted having left, but I also regretted coming back." What is going through your heart and mind as you read that?

→ What are some of the things you regret?

Thoughts, Feelings, Reflections and/or Doodles

CHAPTER 10

Freedom

Don't become defeated and give up.
Become determined and keep going.
Your past does not define your identity nor determine your destiny.
– Becca C. Johnson

Elisa's Story

As the sun came up in the morning, I was high yet finally went to bed. I woke up several hours later, trying to lock the memories of what the men did to me away in a vault that no one could enter. Yet I could feel the burns and bruises on my body, penetrating my mind, making me feel as if I was going crazy.

Crazy that I was still alive.

Crazy that I had ended up in this place.

Crazy that I was trapped here again.

One day, after a particularly bad date, I found myself cleaning the blood off my body for what seemed like the thousandth time. When this man had booked the date, he said that wanted the "girlfriend" experience, but instead, it was a horror show. Just another reason that people couldn't be trusted. *I can't even trust myself.*

Internally, I wanted to scream: *How much more can I survive?*

When AJ found out, he was infuriated that the guy hadn't paid me more money for what he did to me when I was forced to play out his sick fantasies.

"It would've been better if that guy had left you on the side of the road." AJ had a sick sneer on his face as his words pierced me. "At least the vultures could get something valuable out of your worthlessness."

As he spoke, my face was a picture of blankness. I would not let him know that his words were breaking me – that they were piercing the very core of who I thought I was. Despite all the money I made him, he made me feel like a replaceable animal.

What is there to life other than this?

I felt like an old bitch in a body that was broken. By the time I was able to lay down for a nap, my head was spinning and every fiber of my being longed for the numbing power of a fix. Something to catapult me into another existence – even if it meant never waking up again.

Just before I lost consciousness, my mind reminded me of my room at the temporary shelter. I remembered the feeling of being safe. I wanted that again – somehow and in some way. As the numbing haze overtook me and the throes of sleep embraced me, the dream of leaving again was painted across my eyelids.

After that horrible day, I started to think more and more often about leaving. Could I get away again? Could I actually make it through a program? Is exiting worth the hard work it will take to completely start over? Was I only good enough for sex? What was beyond this pain?

During the next few months, whenever I was all alone, which wasn't often, I found myself calling the Human Trafficking Hotline number, the number that was given to me on the street.

Whenever I would call, I would ask to speak to my new "friend" Amy. Amy was the first person I had connected with at the hotline and although she didn't work every day, whenever she was working, she would speak to me so nonjudgmentally, speaking strength and courage into my life. I can't remember the number of times that she told me that I was strong and brave and that I did have the ability to make my own choices.

On the really bad days, I would hang up after talking with Amy, feeling a little bit better and a little closer to potentially leaving, though I was terrified that AJ or the other girls would find out. Consequences were all too real to me.

There was a night where another one of my wifeys didn't come home. Everyone assumed it was like the last time that she had wanted out and ran. We barely thought twice about it until we heard the police found her body in a dumpster the next day behind a hotel. My heart sank with the news. None of us even knew her real name or where she was from. No would be looking for her. Her family, if she had one, might never know she was dead.

I looked around at the girls in the house that day and realized that none of them seemed to care. Would they *care* if it had been me? Or one of them? I care, I thought.

I hated myself. I hated my life. I hated all the things that I have been made to do.

AJ was in his room with a newbie – a young teenage girl who was in love with him, just like I had been when he rescued me. I missed the times that I used to have with him, the times that his arms wrapped around me to make me feel safe and he spoke words of kindness that would engulf me with care and concern.

As the moans of the young girl came through the thin walls, my phone rang, startling me back into the reality of my existence. My heart was beating fast and I had tears falling down my face. But I had to answer in case it was a client.

I answered with my street name, Cherry.

The couple on the other end told me where to go and asked me to come dressed specific to their unique BDSM *(bondage discipline sadism and masochism)* fantasies.

Terror surged through my being.

Fear overtook me.

Anxiety filled me.

The requests this couple made were specific and bold. Bolder than any other call that I had received, which was saying a lot after so many ruthless buyers. These individuals were asking me to do dangerous things and it made me wonder how my body would recover.

Internally, I was shouting *NO*. These calls were the worst, always ending with people receiving sadistic sexual gratification from my own extreme pain. Externally, I heard my voice affirming their requests and repeating the address back to them.

In a dazed state, I gathered my bag and put my coat on. Yet, instead of going in the direction that I knew I needed to go to meet my customers, I found myself going in the opposite direction. After a few steps, I began to run.

My breaths were heavy, yet the air was fresh and made me feel strong. My brain started to clear. AJ won't know for a while. He was all consumed with his grooming process, loving the newbie until she thinks he is her world. As for the couple, *What could they do to me now?*

———————

I call the Hotline number again and they put me on hold for a brief second. When they came back on the phone, they said, "Have you ever heard of Freedom Home?"

Hesitantly I said, "Yes." My voice started to tremble as I asked, "Can you give me their phone number?"

I found myself in a dark alleyway with shadows to hide me from peering eyes, and it was here that I called Freedom Home. "Hi, can you help me?"

The first thing I heard was "Yes, we can help you." As the sound of those five words met my ears, they unlocked a floodgate of tears that I had been holding back since I first found AJ in a room with another girl.

Shaking, I sobbed. I let go.

Although that night seemed to last longer than any other night of my life, for the first time since I was a little girl, a sweet, floral smelling blanket was placed around my shoulders and a soft, older woman asked if she could hold me as I sobbed. She gave me tissues every few minutes and held me as I cried – telling me that I was now safe.

I felt safe.

I was safe.

No one could hurt me there.

Slowly, my sobs stopped and I found my eyes closing with exhaustion. I fell into a fitful sleep.

The next morning, after I woke up, the same lady who had helped me the night before sat with me as I went through all the intake paperwork. The same paperwork that had scared me the day I left the temporary emergency shelter. This time, it didn't seem as daunting. I knew what to expect and I knew that whatever was to come, although terrifying, it wasn't as bad as fearing for my life each day. I didn't feel alone.

Hope sparked within my chest.

Was it possible to heal from everything – including AJ, Damon, Bill, Rudy, and all the tricks – and maybe even see Emmy again? Would she still love me after all I had done and after I had stopped being in her life?

After going through the intake, I fell asleep once more.

Later, I woke up shaking. I felt as if detoxing was destroying my body. I knew I didn't want to go back, but could I really withstand the fix I knew AJ could give me?

The Freedom House staff told me, "It might get worse before it gets better." They were not lying, as every shake in my body from detoxing tempted me to get go back. I often found myself daydreaming about lying in my bed at the house, numb and relaxed by the drugs.

The staff at Freedom Home told me every day that I had value and worth. I found it so hard to believe, as a voice in my head consistently reminded me that I was dirty, stupid, and worthless – hopeless.

As time went on, something deep inside of me kept reminding me about the good times that I had shared with my wifeys. I remembered the way that we could talk about the stupid tricks and somehow find ways to laugh about the silliest things. I remember feeling like I belonged with them, if nowhere else. I remembered the nice items I had: the purses, shoes, lingerie, bath products, makeup. I remembered the drugs that were so readily available– drugs that helped me forget the horrors. But then I remembered someone at Freedom Home telling me, "It is so easy to remember the good things because we so desperately want to forget the past."

One day, in a state of desperation to get away from myself and the staff who didn't understand my haunting memories, I packed my bags. I sat on the edge of my bed, bag in hand, ready to leave. *Could I do it on my own?*

Why do they think it's so much better to talk about things in the past instead of just forgetting them?

Yet, just as I closed the door behind me, I remembered what I was told by the kind lady who had held me the night I arrived. She said, "A day will come when you will want to go back. So you and I are going to make a list of why you left."

At the memory of her voice, a feeling of peace washed over me and a tear gently escaped my eye. "When you are thinking about going back to The Life ... I want you to stop and read this list."

Although a part of me angrily wanted to keep going, a part of me knew I needed to stay. I left the building but found myself sitting on the front steps and pulling out my list.

- *I left because AJ and the buyers never treated me as a human.*

- *I left because I was always being hurt.*

- *I left because AJ kept lying to me and all of the money I made had to go back to him.*

- *I left because I hated the life I was living.*

- *I left because I wasn't allowed to choose the clothes I wore or the food I ate.*

- *I left because I did not know who I was and hated the person I'd become.*

- *I left because the choice of prostitution was really not a choice at all.*

- *I left because I wanted to see Emmy again one day and have her not be ashamed of me.*

As I continued to read my list, the one tear that had escaped soon turned into a steady stream. Sobbing, I walked back into the house. I might not be able to escape the pain but I knew I wanted to escape The Life. Staying was still my best option. (To be continued ...)

Reflections

Elisa decided to stay in the program and stay out of The Life.

We all have times when we doubt our decisions. We wonder if what we're doing is good and we glamorize the bad. We want to forget the past rather than face it. It's a bit like being made to take unpleasant medicine. We know it's supposed to be helpful but find it hard to get past the dreadful taste.

Others have shared, "It's strange being out of The Life, but it's a good kind of strange," "It's harder than I thought it would be (being out) but it doesn't make me want to go back," and, "It's scary, but the hardest and the best decision I've ever made."

Don't be surprised if you feel confused, overwhelmed and out of place at times. You'll eventually feel less "crazy" as you become more and more adjusted. It's then that you can just focus on how thankful you are to be out.

Do you know want to know what makes people feel crazy? Ambivalence. That's when you feel two opposite emotions at the same time. For example, you may both love and hate the controlling person in your life. Or, you might hate the work but love the money and attention. You may be thrilled to be out of The Game yet miss parts of it. Just know that this is *normal*, you're *not* going crazy. Don't be *surprised*; most of what you're thinking and feeling is normal.

Don't be Surprised

Don't be surprised if you ...
   Feel strange and out of place
   Think this new place and people are too good to be true
   Think that it won't last – that is couldn't last
   Are waiting for something bad to happen
Don't be surprised if you ...
   Don't trust the people here
   Don't know what and who to believe
   Feel confused about knowing who's safe and not safe
   Are waiting for someone to hit or hurt you
Don't be surprised if you ...
   Miss the familiar
   Miss your boyfriend
   Miss The Life
   Miss your friends (wife-in-laws)
Don't be surprised if you ...
   Feel scared and unsure about the future
   Don't know what you want to do
   Don't know where to start
   Have a hard time making decisions for yourself
Don't be surprised if you ...
   Feel like a nobody
   Feel insecure
   Feel like you deserve bad things to happen to you
   Feel bad about yourself
Don't be surprised if you ...

Have nightmares

Have flashbacks

Feel anxious and have panic attacks

Feel depressed

Don't be surprised if you ...

Have a hard time trusting people for a while

Are not sure who to trust

Are not sure how to trust

Are not sure when to trust

Don't be surprised if you ... (add to the lists)

Don't be surprised ... it's NORMAL!

BC Johnson, 2011

Identifying Triggers

To truly stay out of The Life, it's helpful to identify what tempts you to think about going back. Most survivors share that the worst trigger for them is calling or seeing people from The Life – whether the controlling person, wifeys or a trick. Others say that craving drugs or when feeling confused or depressed is when they are most vulnerable to thoughts of going back. One survivor wrote, "Money is one of the biggest triggers for me. Nothing sends me into a spiral near depression like being low on money does." For many, when nightmares, panic attacks and other symptoms of complex PTSD (Post-Traumatic Stress Disorder) occur all too frequently, they want to give in rather than keep going on the road to recovery.

What are your temptations and triggers? What makes you most vulnerable to going back? Start making a list. It can help you keep out when you're tempted to go back.

Strengthening Your Decision

When you are triggered, what can you do to strengthen your decision to stay out of The Life? To strengthen your resolve (decision to leave), like Elisa, it helps to go back to the list you made about why you left. This list helps you recall how terrible it was. Do you want to return to that?

Think also about the plans you had for your life before The Life. What old dreams are starting to resurface? What do you want to do now that you're out of The Life? What hopes, goals, and plans do you want to pursue?

One survivor gives this advice: "It's never too late and you deserve to be happy and safe." Other survivors declared, "I LEFT! Good riddance! What took me so long? I'm so glad I FINALLY left. I DID IT!!!"

Survivor Sharing

(Thoughts shared in this section come from people who have been through tough, terrible, traumatic things.)

- *The healing process is not simple or sweet. To heal from trauma one grieves the moments of happiness they didn't have. Healing forces you to rip off protective scabs and pick away at the true cause of infection. It's a bitter process. I want people to understand that it's work, damn hard work to get through and heal from brokenness. I want others to understand that it's OK to be authentic in this struggle because there IS hope ahead.*

  9to20 Blog, August, 2012

- *The first twenty years of my life I was told that I was useless. For some 7,300 days I believed I was useless. But today is not one of those days.*

  Anonymous

When asked, "Who or what helped you get out of The Life?" survivors gave these answers:

- *One day, I just said, "I can't do this anymore."*
- *Believing that help IS available*
- *I went to rehab and didn't go back*
- *Being pregnant*
- *A prostitute's death*
- *After a severe beating*
- *My boyfriend/pimp got jailed*
- *My boyfriend/pimp was killed*
- *Too many arrests*
- *Court helped me get out once and for all*
- *My family being there for me*
- *I was sick and tired of it all and finally came to my senses*
- *I was helped by a trick (buyer)*
- *Getting older*
- *My faith in God*

———————————

Your Story

→ When are you most vulnerable to going back? What people, places, things, events and/or memories trigger thoughts of returning to the life of exploitation? Identify and then avoid them whenever possible.

→ What people, places, things, events, and activities help strengthen your decision to be done with The Life? Make a list of what keeps you strong – what helps your determination to "get out and stay out"?

In Chapter 2 you were asked about your dreams and plans for the future. Let's look at those again:

Before being in The Life (Game) ...

_____I wanted to go to training school to become a _____

.

_____I planned to go to college.

_____I wanted to pursue my dream to become a_____

_____I'd hoped to travel a lot.

_____I wanted to get married and have children.

_____I wanted to help others.

_____I wanted to work with children.

_____I wanted to work with animals.

_____I wanted to: _____

Thoughts, Feelings, Reflections and/or Doodles

CHAPTER 11

Connection

Every success makes you grow strong because it teaches you what to do.
But every failure makes you stronger because it teaches you what not to do.
– Unknown

Elisa's Story

After making my decision to stay at Freedom Home, it was easier for me to see the kindness in the staff, as well as things I never knew I wanted. The staff helped me to see how AJ had groomed me and how he made me into the person he wanted me to be – a money-making puppet in his hands who he made to feel worthless in order to control.

Although life was so much better than what it had been in a long time, it was hard to grieve the losses and fight the lies that I had been told and believed. And, it was hard to trust myself to make my own decisions.

Could I really make good choices now, after so many of my past decisions resulted in so much pain and loss?

AJ had told me what to do, wear, eat, drink, who I was able to talk to and not talk to for so long that it was hard for me to know who I even was. Did I like the color blue because I actually liked it or because it was what he told me he liked me to wear?

I wasn't sure. I was learning.

As I slowly began to learn what I liked and disliked, I also started to build relationships with other survivors.

Jenna was a survivor of familial trafficking. Her dad had started to sell her at a young age. All through school she would go to school during the day and would "work" at night. Her teachers knew something was not right at home, but they had no idea how bad it was. Since coming to Freedom Home, she too was trying to move beyond the traumas that people had inflicted on her.

Hemi had tattoos all over her body. After being sexually abused by her stepdad, she ran away. But then, it got worse. On the streets, she had been used, abused, drug-addicted, sold and exploited for many years before getting into the program.

Then there was Saria, a survivor of gang and labor trafficking. She didn't talk much during our survivor group because she was scared of the repercussions of others hearing her story. But, bit by bit, I could see her working to embrace the beautiful future she was beginning to envision. I would watch the incredible things she could make with her hands. She focused so completely on whatever she was creating. I would watch and my heart would ache, as it would bring a rush of memories of Emmy sitting at the kitchen table back in our little apartment, focusing so intently on a math problem, or a spelling word.

I missed Emmy with every beat of my heart, but all I could do was hope that she was safe.

As the other survivors began to share, I learned that there were other types of trafficking taking place, including trafficking of boys, illicit massage parlors and nail salons, domestic servitude, and so much more. It was incredible to realize other people had to go through what I had gone through.

I was not alone.

———————

Although I was free and was experiencing moments of genuine, deep happiness for the first time in years, I would still have to fight off thoughts of returning to The Life.

But even those slowly began to change.

When I first arrived, I had had to fight thoughts of returning daily. Soon it changed into a weekly battle. After a while, I began to only think about going back when I found myself getting super stressed or tired.

I was told that this was normal, which helped me to feel less worthless for being tempted to go back. Instead of hiding these feelings, I was learning to invite my mentors and therapist into those feelings and experiences. Once they knew, they were able to talk me through it and fight it. The first time they told me that I no longer had to fight anything by myself again, I didn't believe them. But over and over again they showed me through their actions that they were truly on my team. I had never had a team before.

I was relieved.

Secrets had weighed down on me my entire life. Rudy, Bill, AJ – I had kept my screams as well as my stories buried so deep, that it felt so freeing to finally speak them out, let them all go, and feel the weight leave me.

At Freedom Home, I was repeatedly told that I was brave and strong. The staff told me, almost on a daily basis, "We believe in you!"

I carried their words close to my heart.

I was required to attend a 12-step Narcotics Anonymous (NA) group. I was skeptical and apprehensive about going, but found it to be incredibly helpful, more than I could have ever guessed. The NA meetings helped give me the opportunity to gain freedom from addiction, which always led me back to my boyfriend pimp. I began to believe I could stay sober, to believe I could have a real life.

I am strong.

In that group I met others who had similar experiences to mine. They were also trying to get out and stay out but were living on their own and attending what they called a "mentoring, case-management program." From them I learned that there are other programs that can come alongside survivors and help them navigate independent and safe living and include helpful, intensive classes.

In addition to going to NA, I attended weekly individual counseling, group counseling, and a mentor-survivor group. I was learning more about myself and was starting to feel empowered. It was still super hard at times – especially when my therapist asked me to go deeper into the lies that I had believed about myself my whole life.

I had believed for so long that AJ was loving and kind, rather than the truth that he had groomed me from the beginning to pimp me out. He had planned to hurt and sell me. This truth always cut my heart like a knife, but I needed to acknowledge it if I was going to reject all the other lies that he wanted me to believe about myself.

I cried a lot those days. My therapist said that is a sign of healing, a release of all I was letting go of as I began to embrace something new. It was safe to cry. Crying wasn't bad, it wasn't a sign of weakness as I had always believed.

Crying became my strength.

The staff members always encouraged me and reminded me that I was so much braver than I had ever imagined.

I finally got my ID card and began to attend the local community college. I felt like I was so far behind everyone else my age. I had never been to college or even held a job.

Not only had I lost so much education to AJ and Damon, but I realized even my time in school growing up was so overshadowed by my need to protect Emmy, that I had never been fully present in school and had missed so much.

I had so much to learn.

Every day, I encountered moments and things that made me feel so dumb. I wanted to curl up on myself with shame and embarrassment or hide from the world.

But I had learned to remind myself of my own strength and resilience.

I may feel stupid sometimes, but I am not stupid.

Entering college for the first time was terrifying.

I worked harder than I ever had in my life, so when my first exam was returned and I barely passed, my heart sunk with disappointment.

I walked into dinner that evening with my spirits so low, but soon found myself crying as the staff gave me flowers and everyone in the room cheered. They said they were celebrating how hard I had worked. They didn't see me as a failure, they saw me as strong and resilient. I felt so much love and hope bubbling in my chest as joyful tears streamed down my cheeks.

Maybe I can actually succeed in life.

Slowly, I began to feel like a human – not just an animal to be used and abused for the sexual pleasures of others.

I have dignity and worth now.

The dreams I had as a little girl began to surge through my being in a new way. The dreams were slightly different now, yet somehow even more beautiful than before. These dreams were built on freedom and possibility – my freedom.

Every new experience that I had propelled me into the creation of new memories. Although it was still hard, I believed the truth that my past did not need to define my future.

Recently, I reconnected with my mother. It was both hard and good. We were never close, and still are not, but she recently told me, "I am proud of you." When I was trying to protect Emmy, I had longed to hear those words. They came years later than I had hoped and expected, but they came.

I had yet to tell my mom what Bill did to me, but my therapist and I were talking about different ways for me to tell her. One day I would find the words to share and express that pain to her.

In addition to connecting with my mom, I was finally able to reconnect with Emmy.

She was not mad at me. She still loved me.

Although I had hurt her when I stopped being in her life, she understood and Freedom Home helped educate her on sexual exploitation and trafficking.

The first time I saw her, I burst into tears. I loved her more than anything in the world and I knew the moment I saw her that I would never go back to The Life if it took me away from her again.

She had grown up so much. She was a beautiful young lady now and so incredibly smart. We talked about moving in together when I finish my program, and I couldn't imagine anything I would love more.

I eventually shared my story with Emmy. We both cried and cried. Then, she turned to me and said, "Thank you for protecting me. But now, maybe we can start protecting each other."

I woke up one day to realize I liked my life. If it weren't for Freedom Home, I might not have even made it to today. They celebrated my successes and helped me grow from my failures, empowering me to make my own decisions. Life's not perfect, I have ups and downs, but now I know I never have to go back to the way things were. I now have tools to help me move forward beyond my past and painful memories.

I am proud of the person that I have become.

I found out after I arrived at Freedom Home that they were faith-based. This was initially off-putting for me, because I had some pastors and "churchgoers" who found sanctuary in my body – which led me to wrongfully believe that God wasn't any better. Yet, the staff never pressured me to accept their beliefs about God. Rather, I was told, "It's your life and choice, your spirituality and your faith." Slowly, my heart began to change and I wanted to know more about who God is and actually form a healthy relationship with him." Spirituality has been important to my healing.

I cannot imagine ever going back to The Life.

I am free. (To be continued ...)

Reflections

Showing Elisa authentic compassion and safe love, the people at Freedom Home are helping her face both the hard memories of her past and the new experiences of the future. Elisa is learning many new things and in every choice she makes, she takes another step toward her freedom and healing.

Just like Elisa, as you get stronger, you too can realize that you're not a bad person. You have skills other than satisfying customers. You can discover (or rediscover) your interests, likes and dislikes, your talents and abilities. And best of all, as the truth sinks in, you can dare to dream again.

Yet, for now, you need to focus on believing, really believing the truth. Oftentimes we are our own worst enemies and our harshest critic. It is time to stop beating yourself up.

We believe that as you continue to take steps forward, you will get stronger and stronger. You will see change happen, sometimes more slowly than you wish and other times faster than you think you can handle – but you can. You are worth so much more than the abuse, rapes, and violence you have endured.

Transferable Skills

Most of those who transition away from The Life feel discouraged about the future, thinking "I'm not good at anything. I have no skills." But, that's not true. The following list shows what we call transferable skills, skills that you most likely gained in The Life that can now be used to help you get a job in another industry.

Skills and Strengths

- adaptable

- alert and aware

- can read people easily (perceptive)

- can think on your feet
- cleanliness
- communication skills (good listening/talking skills)
- computer skills
- creative
- determination and perseverance
- flexible/adaptable, good under stress
- good at handling difficult people
- good customer service
- loyal and hardworking
- money handling skills
- physical stamina, endurance, fit, fighter
- problem-solving skills
- recruitment skills
- sales, promotion and marketing skills

We know it is still hard to see good in things that are overwhelming, especially when you are needing to take these transferable skills to write a resume and get a job. The reality is others have done it and you can do it too.

You don't need to hustle anymore, to prove yourself or to please someone else. You just need to commit to a gradual process of growth – which facilitates more growth and develops a greater ability to overcome adversity in the future.

Survivor Sharing

(Thoughts shared in this section come from people who have been through tough, terrible, traumatic things.)

- *You have bigger and better things waiting for you outside of The Life.*

    Anonymous

- *You are worth so much more than you may believe. You deserve so much more than how you've been treated.*

    JH

- *If you feel unworthy, just know that God says otherwise.*

    AW

- *It is possible and you have us, survivor sisters and others, who will help you if you want help.*

    Anonymous

- *There are always options for you, and people (even strangers) who care about you.*

    Anonymous

- *After I got out, I found a job, got married and began a family.*

    Anonymous

- *When I got out and stayed out, I started working with an organization to help battered and exploited women like I was.*

    Anonymous

- *I got free, really free of drugs when I got out. I'm three years sober now.*

    Anonymous

- *Once I got out and dealt with all of the court records, I was able to get my children back.*

  Anonymous

- *Counseling helps and having a healthy community helps.*

- *I fight daily to not dwell on what was lost but instead to focus on what I can make new today. Today is a new day and today has all the potential in the world of being a good day.*

  9to20 Blog, October, 2011

- *When I got out and got clean, I went back to school, finished my GED and then went on to study at the local college.*

  Anonymous

Your Story

→ Write down your own list of transferable skills that you could potentially use in another industry?

→ In what ways have you grown over the past few years?

I'm Over It! Checklist

Here's a checklist to help you evaluate how you're doing on the road to recovery. There's no magic number of checked items that declares you are "over it" but the more the better. Simply check all that describe you now. This is to help you see how far you've come and also to help you identify what else you need to work on. Track your progress by going through the checklist again every few months. Don't beat yourself up, some back and forth of recovery is to be expected. Maybe an item that you thought you had already moved past is now showing up again.

Remember, recovery can be messy, with some steps forward, along with some steps backward. That's to be expected and doesn't mean you're failing. The main thing is that you are continuing to move forward and not giving up. Eventually, you will have more steps forward than backward.

Here's How I'm Doing (My Self-Evaluation):

_____ 1. I rarely, if ever, think about going back.

_____ 2. I see myself as a victim and a survivor.

_____ 3. Although I may still wonder, I know that he/she never really loved me, at least not in a healthy way.

_____ 4. I've recognized what behaviors and attitudes I developed in order to survive and am trying to keep the good but get rid of the bad parts.

_____ 5. I don't find myself wanting to call him anymore.

_____ 6. I think more about the future than I dwell on the past.

_____ 7. Even when I'd love to make some quick money, I never seriously consider going back.

_____ 8. I don't beat myself up as much anymore but can see my strengths, skills and abilities.

_____ 9. I know what triggers me and/or makes me feel worse.

_____ 10. I know what people, place & things are temptations to me and avoid them.

_____ 11. I do things I enjoy, for myself, not just to please someone else.

_____ 12. I am able to express my emotions without withdrawing or blowing up all the time.

_____ 13. I'm learning to trust other people.

_____ 14. I've shared my story with another person.

_____ 15. I've gotten a lot better at not believing all the lies in my head.

_____ 16. I'm not in survival mode all the time.

_____ 17. When I feel down, I seek people to talk to and do activities that make me feel better.

_____ 18. I'm learning to communicate what I'm thinking and feeling rather than bottle it up.

_____ 19. I'm allowing myself to feel rather than numbing my emotions.

_____ 20. I've gotten professional help (counseling) to work through some of the deeper issues.

_____ 21. I've learned to laugh and find happiness in little and big things.

_____ 22. Although I miss certain things about The Life, I'm glad I'm out once and for all.

_____ 23. I try not to glamorize The Life but remember the bad stuff too (chaos, violence, abuse).

_____ 24. I realize that the child abuse that happened to me was not my fault.

_____ 25. I'm working on forgiving myself for my bad choices and what I did to others.

_____ 26. I try to take care of myself – exercise, diet, rest ...

_____ 27. I have friends and/or a support group that I can talk with.

___ 28. I've made peace with God (Higher Power).

___ 29. I've been clean and sober for quite a while now (2+ years).

___ 30. I'm learning how to recognize safe, healthy people.

___ 31. I now understand codependency and am trying to avoid it in relationships.

___ 32. I'm working on forgiveness because I don't want people or the past to control me nor do I want to become a bitter, negative person.

___ 33. I know that what happened to me doesn't define who I am or determine my destiny.

Becca C. Johnson, Ph.D., 2015

Thoughts, Feelings, Reflections and/or Doodles

CHAPTER 12

The Future

"No one is useless in this world who lightens the burdens of another."
— Charles Dickens
"When your only competition is becoming a better you, you will always win."
— Jackie Griffin

Elisa's Story

A year has passed since I graduated from Freedom Home. I am now living with my sister Emmy. We love living together. She is doing so well and is working full time as an elementary school teacher.

Through the help of therapists, we have learned how to communicate with each other in a way that respects our unique personalities.

It's been fun to see how outgoing Emmy is – she loves to hang out with people, while I love the quietness of our home and the stability of a schedule that stays the same. Some people call Emmy extroverted and me introverted, but I personally like to say that we are just embracing our needs, which Freedom Home taught me is healthy and OK. We don't need to change to make anyone else happy.

After finishing my associate degree at our local college, I began working with children at a local preschool. It has been so life-giving and healing to be able to see life through the innocence of these kids. They embody so much energy and joy. I always tell them what the staff members at Freedom Home told me, "You are strong, brave, and perfect just the way you are – you don't need to change anything for me to care about you." They smile when I say this and seem to believe me. I find that the more I say it out loud, the more that I remember my own beautiful strength.

For fun, I love going outside, running and regularly volunteering at the humane society, a place where wounded and abused animals are loved and nursed back to health. With each animal I hold, I find myself whispering into their ears, "If I can heal, you can too." Some part of me believes they actually understand what I say. Or maybe they just understand the feeling of hope.

I used to think that I had nothing to offer or give others, but I am now seeing meaningful ways that I can give back to others every day.

———

It's really interesting to see what my survivor sisters from Freedom Home are doing. Although we went through the same program, each of us are doing different things.

Jenna is now the survivor mentor at an anti-trafficking nonprofit in another state. She always had a heart for wanting to help others move from being a victim to a thriver. She wants other individuals who have been exploited to experience freedom. Her involvement has been invaluable because she is able to inform the organization of how to best reach and help those caught in sexual exploitation. She is giving hope to others too.

Hemi discovered that she loves art – and is good at it. She's working at a tattoo shop where she creates amazing designs. She also helps cover up or change old, unwanted tattoos, into pleasing works of art. I thought, *That's just like what God does with us, takes our brokenness and makes something beautiful out of us.*

Saria is now married. She met her husband at a church. He's amazing. I was in their wedding party as a bridesmaid. From what I have observed, he treats her with so much respect. They are now expecting their first child and are so thrilled. I have never seen her sparkle with such excitement and I don't think it's just the baby glow – rather, I think she is really happy with her new life. I am going to be helping them paint the nursery soon.

I don't know if I will ever get married, but through watching her and other safe men in my life, for the first time I am starting to believe that real love is possible – love that is gentle, kind, and safe.

When intrusive, depressive, and negative thoughts invade my mind, I fight back with truth statements. Like, I have a purpose. *Sex does not define me. I have a beautiful future ahead of me. I am smart. I am worth protecting.*

Life is still hard at times, but even people who haven't been through what I have been through experience hard times too. This is normal and part of being human.

I remind myself, "I am a tough fighter." *A very tough fighter.*

A smile tugs at my lips. I am so much stronger than I ever imagined.

I like the person I am becoming.

If I can do it, you can do it too.

Reflections

Elisa has not only graduated from community college, but she is living with her sister, Emmy, and has a fulfilling life. Although difficulties come up, she loves what she is doing now and is thriving (some people prefer the words thriver or overcomer instead of survivor).

Here it is important to recognize, that you, just like Elisa, have so much to offer the world. You are valuable and important. Your past does not define you any longer!

One part of thriving is seeing beyond our own pain. If you are struggling to know where to start, we would love to encourage you to look beyond the walls of your own self and seek to give kindness to others. This process might look like volunteering at a humane shelter, volunteering at a soup kitchen, or smiling at a child who looks sad. There are so many possibilities and you get to choose what is best for you and your needs.

We also want you to know that you do not have to help fight sexual exploitation nor tell your story – unless you want to. Even if you are thankful to a person or program for helping you get out and grow, you do not have to publicly share. It's your story to tell if and when you choose. You may feel pressure to say "yes" to sharing but it should be your choice. Once you share publicly, your story becomes known and accessible to anyone, so make the decision carefully regarding whether or not to share.

What happened to you is only part of your life's story. The rest has yet to be written. Your past doesn't have to define your identity or determine your destiny.

Finally, we know that you are used to surviving and toughing it out on your own, but you need people. We all need safe people in our lives – whether friends, family, support groups, or professional counselors. Numbing and not trusting have been part of your life, but now is the time to let go of those bad habits. Now's the time to fully embrace your potential and possibilities. You have so much life ahead!

Survivor Sharing

(Thoughts shared in this section come from people who have been through tough, terrible, traumatic things.)

- *There is nothing that you've done, no matter how bad it is, that you can't overcome. The world that you see from the outside looking in, that you long to be in, is not out of your reach. There is hope and there is help if you're honest, open and willing for a different life.*

  JH 6/16

- *All the traffickers and pimps out there are the ones who first instilled the lies in my heart. Yet I now know the Truth. I'm worth more than a life of prostitution.*

Anonymous

Your Story

→ List the names and phone numbers of several safe support people.

→ What does giving back to others mean to you? (Volunteering, helping, sharing, giving ...)

→ What statements, thoughts, ideas ... do you want to remember from this book? What were most helpful to you?

Thoughts, Feelings, Reflections and/or Doodles

RESOURCES: Where to Get Help

Hotlines

Human Trafficking hotline – National Human Trafficking Resource Center (NHTRC)

24-hour Hotline:

1-888-373-7888

Domestic Violence – National Domestic Violence Hotline

24-hour Hotline:

1-800-799-SAFE (7233)

Sexual Abuse – Rape, Abuse and Incest National Network (RAINN)

24-hour Hotline:

1-800-656-4673

National Suicide Prevention Lifeline

24-hour Hotline:

1-800-273-TALK (8255)

National Runaway Switchboard

1-800-786-2929

National Center for Missing and Exploited Children Missingkids.org

24-hour call center:

1-800-THE-LOST (1-800-843-5678)

To report child sexual exploitation use our CyberTipline®.

To report information about a missing child call

1-800-THE-LOST (1-800-843-5678).

Office for Victims of Crime, Directory of Crime Victim Services. victimsofcrime.org

Go to website for a directory of offices in your area

http://www.victimsofcrime.org/help-for-crime-victims/national-hotlines-and-helpful-links

Anti-Human Trafficking Organizations

There are now thousands of anti-trafficking and other helpful organizations. For overall information, go to GlobalSlaveryIndex.org and HumanTraffickingHotline.org. The following list includes but a few of the many organizations.

Survivor-Led Anti-Trafficking Organizations

BridgeHope   www.BridgeHopeNow.org

BridgeHope exists to bring awareness to the realities of exploitation, combat vulnerability with technology, and facilitate an environment where survivors of exploitation can thrive. BridgeHope created both the GiveHope holiday program for survivors around the US.

Breaking Free breakingfree.net

Every year, Breaking Free helps hundreds of women escape sex trafficking and prostitution through direct services. It provide housing, advocacy, intensive education programs, support, and hope to survivors. Breaking Free's own diversity helps to intentionally provide additional support to serve women of color who are disproportionately represented in the demographics of sex trafficking, prostitution, and sexual exploitation.

Rebecca Bender Initiative   rebeccabender.org, elevate-academy.org

Rebecca Bender Initiative exists to see a world free from exploitation. With a desire to see survivors thrive, RBI founded Elevate Academy, the largest online resource for survivors of human trafficking in 2014. Offering courses, mentoring, professional coaching, and more, Elevate Academy assists students in healing, job readiness, and economic empowerment, enabling them to become truly self-sustainable. Additionally, RBI's Equip program provides in-depth training to law enforcement, medical personnel, advocates, and professionals nationwide on identifying and responding to human trafficking in their communities.

GEMS – Girls Educational and Mentoring Service   gems-girls.org

GEMS'S mission is to empower girls and young women, ages 12–24, who have experienced commercial sexual exploitation and domestic trafficking to exit the commercial sex industry and develop to their full potential. GEMS is committed to ending commercial sexual exploitation and domestic trafficking by changing individual lives, transforming public perception and revolutionizing the systems and policies that impact commercially sexually exploited youth.

OPS – Organization for Prostitution Survivors   seattleops.org

OPS accompanies survivors of prostitution in creating and sustaining efforts to heal from and end this practice of gender-based violence. Their survivor support hotline operates Monday–Fridays, 10 a.m. until 6 p.m.

Recovery Support Programs

Alliance Referral System   shelteredalliance.org/ARS

The National Trafficking Sheltered Alliance endeavors to expedite placement of victims into qualified programs that have availability. We have identified 170+ residential service providers, the majority of them are able to take referrals from anywhere in the U.S. – we just have to close the gap between the victim seeking placement and the agencies who can offer services. The Alliance Referral System (ARS) is open to any referring agency who has encountered a victim of domestic human trafficking, sexual exploitation, or prostitution, and who is seeking residential care.

Elevate Academy elevate-academy.org   (see also Rebecca Bender Initiative)

This specialized online school provides support and education so survivors of human trafficking can heal, thrive and pursue their dreams. Elevate is currently serving students across the U.S. and in nine countries around the world and offers 100 percent tuition assistance. With the support of partners and donors, Elevate Academy gives students a safe online space to learn, connect, heal and thrive.

REST: Real Escape from the Sex Trade – Seattle, WA iwantrest.com

REST offers pathways to freedom, safety, and hope to individuals who have experienced the sex trade. Programs include: 24/7 hotline: (206) 451-7378, low-barrier emergency shelter (up to 90 days), drop-in center, integrated health clinic, intensive case management, Economic and Leadership Empowerment Academy, and transitional home (up to 2 years). REST believes that everyone deserves to be loved. Everyone deserves a life free from exploitation.

Engedi Refuge   endgedirefuge.com

Engedi Refuge is a place of safety and healing for victims of sex trafficking. It provides a comprehensive and therapeutic long-term residential program which includes safe housing, case management, life skills training, classroom curriculum and individual, trauma-focused counseling. These are all designed to empower the women to have the best possible chance to permanently remove themselves from exploitation and experience a healthy, fulfilling life.

Awareness, Advocacy, Policy and Partnerships

Polaris   polarisproject.org

We use what we learn to pilot big, new ideas for slowly, carefully, finally, dismantling big, old systems that make trafficking possible. We are focused where we think we can make the most change: systems that trap impoverished migrants in degrading conditions; systems that allow sex traffickers to hide behind screens and systems that, if optimized, would allow the financial services industry to use traffickers' own money to shut them down.

Shared Hope   sharedhope.org

Shared Hope International strives to prevent the conditions that foster sex trafficking, restore victims of sex slavery, and bring justice to vulnerable women and children. We envision a world passionately opposed to sex trafficking and a community committed to restoring survivors to lives of purpose, value and choice – one life at a time.

Exodus Cry   exoduscry.com

Exodus Cry is committed to abolishing sex trafficking and breaking the cycle of commercial sexual exploitation while assisting and empowering its victims. Our work involves uprooting the underlying causes in our culture that allow the industry of sexual exploitation to thrive and helping those who have been sexually exploited.

Rescue Freedom International   rescuefreedom.org

Rescue:Freedom International is on a mission to end slavery around the world. They exist to empower the rescue and restoration of those in sexual slavery and to prevent exploitation. Rescue:Freedom works through Local Partners - organizations that are fighting sexual slavery in their local community. RFI partners with organizations that demonstrate programmatic effectiveness, financial accountability, and an expert level understanding of slavery.

RESOURCES: Books

While there are many, many books now written by and about survivors of abuse, violence and exploitation and also about the healing journey, listed here are but a few.

For Victims and Those Who Want to Understand and Help

Girls Like Us – Fighting for a World Where Girls are Not for Sale, an Activist Finds Her Calling and Heals Herself by Rachel Lloyd, 2011, HarperCollins

In Pursuit of Love: One Woman's Journey from Trafficked to Triumphant by Rebecca Bender, 2020, Zondervan

Paid For – My Journey through Prostitution by Rachel Moran, 2013, W.W. Norton & Company

The Journey to Hope – Overcoming Abuse by Becca C. Johnson, 2018 (available through Amazon.com; for the Spanish version, order via DrBeccaJohnson@gmail.com)

What Happened to Me?! – Healing for Sex Trafficking Survivors by Toni McKinley, LPC, 2018 (available through Amazon.com)

For Those Who Want to Understand and Help

In Our Backyard – Human Trafficking in America and What We Can Do to Stop It by Nita Belles, 2013, Baker Books

Renting Lacy – A Story of America's Prostituted Children, A Call to Action by Linda Smith with Cindy Coloma, 2009, Shared Hope International (www.SharedHope.org)

Somebody's Daughter: The Hidden Story of America's Prostituted Children and the Battle to Save Them by Julian Sher, 2013, Chicago Review Press

The Journey to Hope – Overcoming Abuse by Becca C. Johnson, 2018 (available through Amazon.com; for the Spanish version, order via DrBeccaJohnson@gmail.com)

APPENDICES

Appendix A

What about Familial Trafficking?
(from a survivor's perspective)

Appendix B

MY Thoughts and Feelings about The Life
(used to gather survivor insight)

Appendix C

Questions about The Life
(used to gather survivor insight)

Appendix D

About the 9to20 Blog Author

Appendix E

More about the Authors

Appendix A

What about Familial Trafficking?

(a survivor's perspective)

When people first hear about familial sex trafficking, they usually give a staggered and shocked response. "What? How can that be? How can a family member sell their child?" I then have to explain that, unfortunately, it not only happens, but it is also not uncommon. In fact, it happened to me.

If you have turned to this section, perhaps you too have experienced the deep pain and trauma of familial trafficking. My friend, you are not alone.

Understanding Familial Trafficking

Something that has helped me in my recovery process is learning what familial trafficking is. It is exploitation perpetrated by a family member—a parent, older sibling, aunt, uncle, cousin, or grandparent. Similar to other forms of abuse, trafficking and exploitation, the tactics of coercion, force, and fraud are used to make the child do sexual activities with others for profit or gain.

Everyone's story is different. One survivor of family trafficking told me that she was first sold at age five to her brother's friends. Another victim was first sexually abused by his father at age two then told to allow other men to do the same. A young girl was sold to her grandfather's friends, then others. For some, it began during puberty when their body changed from that of a child to a developing teenager. Others have been unable to voice what happened but communicate the immense pain clearly through their tears.

Familial trafficking does not fit into a specific mold. Layers of shame and silence develop, making it difficult for individuals to recognize and respond. For instance, you might have grown up in a well-respected family within your community. You may have thought, "No one would believe the horrors experienced." Or perhaps you grew up in a rural community without knowing that other family relationships and realities existed. Friend, victims of familial trafficking are found in all types of families—rich or poor, big and small, young and old, and from all types of ethnic and religious backgrounds and geographic areas.

I do not know your story, but as I have worked with many survivors from around the world, some common reasons why familial trafficking takes place include:

- *Desperation/Poverty:* Poverty can lead people to do things they might not do if they had other choices. In desperation, a guardian might initiate the sale of a child to be able to buy food, pay rent, or provide medical care for a loved one.

- *Addictions/Drugs:* Some familial trafficking takes place to support the parent or perpetrator's substance abuse addiction.

- *Ritual/Religious:* Some familial trafficking happens in cults, rituals, and other deviant religious practices by family members. Pledges, blood oaths, sacrifices, guilt, and other methods of obtaining victim silence are common and contain multiple layers of confusing messages.

- *Money/Greed:* Unfortunately, many people lust after the financial gain possible in selling their family member. They view the minor as a money-making machine—a way to get ahead or as a way to not work themselves. The relationship that should be based on love is replaced by greed.

- *Sexual Gratification:* Many victims are first sexually abused by a family perpetrator who seeks to fulfill their own selfish sexual desires. This evolves into selling the minor to others and may include voyeurism and pornography as well for the perpetrator's arousal and continued sexual fantasies.

- *Community Status:* Sometimes, familial trafficking is used as a means to gain status within an illicit community.

Ultimately, the common denominator of all familial trafficking is the fact that it changes how a child perceives what is normal, who is safe, and how to live life freely. The people that should have taken care of and protected the child are the very same people who are perpetrating the pain of betrayal. The healing process is difficult, painful, and uncertain. How does one begin to heal when the very process of love, trust, and attachment is the thing that was used against them?

The coercion experienced in familial exploitation looks different than in other forms of trafficking, yet equally wrong. Whether a boyfriend as in Elisa's story, one's gang "family," one's biological or adoptive family or other forms of exploitation, it is all not okay, not normal, not right. No matter what was used against you or how it was used against you, it was not your fault. And now, it is okay to walk away and walk toward joy, hope, and freedom.

The Bond of Family

Personally, I think one of the hardest things about familial trafficking is the strong bond we feel to stay connected to people who have perpetrated so much pain against us. We might want to leave so desperately, and yet something unseen holds us back. For some survivors, it might be the anxiety of being all alone, the fear that threats will become a reality, or that it will be our fault if the family system breaks down after we get away. For other survivors, it might be the fact that our abusers won't leave us alone. We may think that the only way to deal with the abusers is to maintain a relationship, even though it triggers us like crazy and keeps us captive to the secrets of the past.

My friend, I know it is so very hard. If you are reading this right now, you might be experiencing a multitude of contrasting feelings. Your feelings are valid, and your pain is not forgotten. It is challenging for us to leave (or stay disconnected from family). It is okay to create a new family determined and defined by you. It is okay to stay away from those who hurt you. It is okay to walk away and walk into the big and scary world and to embrace it. It will be hard, but remember, your past does not define your future!

I care about you so very much!

Your friend,
Jessa

Appendix B

My Thoughts and Feelings about The Life

Please complete the sentences below. Don't worry about spelling or grammar or what others will think. There are NO right or wrong answers. Just write what you honestly think and feel. Use the back side or another sheet of paper if you want more space to write.

1. I miss The Life when

_____

2. What I DON'T miss is

_____

3. My boyfriend

_____

4. I'm glad I left The Life when I think about

_____

5. I often ask myself

_____

6. I wish I could

_____

7. I'm glad I didn't

_____

8. I need

_____

9. I wish people wouldn't

_____

10. I am most afraid

_____

11. I get sad when

_____

12. Sometimes I feel like

_____

13. When I think about the future I

_____

14. I think it is important

_____

15. If I could do anything, I would

_____

16. I don't like it when

_____

17. I am stronger than before because

_____

18. My family

_____

19. I get mad when

_____

20. I think about going back to The Life when

_____

21. I felt hopeless when

_____

22. I hate it when

_____

23. Now I know that The Life

_____

24. When others tell me "It wasn't your fault," I

_____

25. I'm happiest when

_____

Comments:

Name (birth name / "street" name?)		Age			
Today's date		Birthdate			
Gender preference	Male	Female	LGBTQ+		Other
Age entered The Life		Age left The Life			
# times left The Life (then returned)					
How long have you been OUT of The Life?					
Days	Weeks		Months		Years
Can we use your comments to help others?					
Yes			No		
Do you want us to use **your name** or make it **anonymous**?					
If "your name," what name or initials do you want us to use?					

Appendix C

Questions about The Life

We are putting together a booklet to encourage those in The Life to get out and for those out of The Life to stay out. Your answers will be helpful as we all seek to help those who seem stuck. THANK YOU!

1. **When you were in The Life, did you think much about getting out?**
   (check one and share your thoughts)

   ❏ never
   ❏ hardly ever
   ❏ sometimes

   ❏ most of the time
   ❏ a lot at first, then gave up
   ❏ constantly

2. **When did you first think about getting out?**
   (check those that apply then explain)

   ❏ right away
   ❏ after a few months
   ❏ after a long time (__# of years)

   ❏ never thought about it (didn't cross my mind that I could have any other kind of life)
   ❏ never thought about it (didn't think escape was possible)

3. **When did you think most about leaving?**
   (check those that apply then share why)

   ❏ after a beating
   ❏ after an especially horrible night with johns or a bad trick

   ❏ when missing my family
   ❏ when he'd go with someone else and not me

   For me, it was:

4. **What did you LIKE the most about being in The Life?**

5. **Why did you STAY?**
   (check ALL that apply then share your thoughts)

   ❏ enjoyed the attention
   ❏ enjoyed the "glamour"
   ❏ enjoyed clothes & material things
   ❏ afraid of getting hurt
   ❏ nothing to go to
   ❏ felt like "shit" – no one would want me
   ❏ nowhere to go
   ❏ no one to go to

   ❏ believed no one would help me
   ❏ believed no one could help me
   ❏ drug addiction
   ❏ I was in love
   ❏ getting to travel
   ❏ power & control
   ❏ money

   For me, it was:

6. What did you HATE about being in The Life?
(check ALL that apply then share your thoughts)

- being beaten, kicked
- the continual lies
- having to give up the money I made
- being told what to do
- no freedom
- the deception & betrayal
- selling my body
- johns
- being "raped" over & over

- having to beat others
- feeling like "shit"
- having to do porn acts
- moving around a lot
- dirty hotels
- having to lie
- the shame
- feeling dirty

For me, it was:

7. What kept you from LEAVING The Life?

8. What or Who helped you decide to LEAVE The Life?
(check ALL that apply then share)

- a friend
- fellow "prostitute"
- a john
- being pregnant
- prostitute's death
- religion/faith
- police/law
- severe beating/trauma
- belief that help WAS

- available
- family
- sick & tired
- too many arrests
- death scare
- boyfriend jailed/killed
- came to my senses
- a book I read

For me, it was:

9. **How often do you think about or are you tempted to RETURN to The Life?**

   (check & share thoughts)

   ❑ every minute/hour
   ❑ daily
   ❑ weekly
   ❑ once every few weeks

   ❑ around once a month
   ❑ rarely
   ❑ never

10. **What or who helped you get out once and for all?**

11. **What ADVICE ON GETTING OUT would you give to those in The Life?**

12. **Anything else you would like to share to encourage others to LEAVE and STAY OUT of The Life?**

13. About Me

I was in The Life for_____ # of

| Weeks | Months | Years |

I have been out of The Life for_____ # of

| Weeks | Months | Years |

❑ I give permission for my written answers (& any other given
   information) to be used to help others get out of The Life.

OR

❑ Yes, but please don't use my name. I want it to be
   anonymous (please initial)_____

OR

❑ Yes, but please use the following name: __ _____
   (please initial) _____

OR

❑ I would like to be acknowledged (cited). IF so, please print
   then sign your name below:

| Name Printed | | Name Signed | |

LEAVING THE LIFE

Appendix D

About the 9to20 Blog Author

9to20.wordpress.com

I'm willing to take the risk if you are – to become uncomfortable. I'm willing to share with you my story of being sexually trafficked right here in America, if you're willing to listen. What I do not want, however, is for this to be a story of despair – because it's not. It's a story of hope. There is a thrasher-filled road of healing ahead of me, yes, but I am in the process of freedom.

May this blog serve as an education to those who do not yet know or understand the atrocities of trafficking and may it serve as encouragement to those who understand it all too well.

I grew up in the suburbs of a town just a little smaller than one hundred thousand people. I was a straight-A student who worshipped the ground her big brother walked on, as he was often my defender from a physically and sexually abusive father and my relief from an emotionally unstable mother.

When I was eight my brother left for college and the dynamic of our household changed dramatically.

My father had lost yet another job and he and my mother turned to me as a steadier source of income. I will never forget that day. The way it turned my stomach so sick, the way the men's semen smelled on my body ... so foreign and sour. It lingered for hours. This first time I was sold for sex, it was to multiple men at once. I was nine years old.

For the next eleven years of my life, I was forced to have sex with hundreds of men. I was hit, mocked, urinated upon and exploited in the backs of trucks, corner markets, cheap hotels, my own bedroom and on the Internet.

*Every touch and ugly word only added to the lie that sex was all I had to offer. It was my "duty" because **I was nothing more than a whore.** There was no one I could trust and certainly no one who could help or believe me. After all, I deserved this – or so I thought.*

In order to cope, I had convinced myself that it was all a choice and ignored the fact that I was enslaved. I ran away several times but always went back – there was simply nowhere else for me to go. My parents had me told me repeatedly that either they would kill me or if I did make it to someone who could help, that those people wouldn't believe a word I would say. Nothing in my life so far had shown me that they were lying.

Looking back now, I see that there might have been someone who would have believed me if I had come outright with it all. Several times I alluded to teachers or other people in positions of authority that some kind of abuse was taking place but I was simply too scared to say anything more. I would instead just throw out a pathetic phrase here or there and beg the universe to read in between the lines to save my sanity. Thank you, Jesus, that today I am free.

9to20 Blog, October, 2011

What I am is a broken individual, healed by the grace of God and passionate about fighting the prevalence of sexual abuse. I am a survivor of despair and doubt. I am a survivor of humiliation and lies, of violence and rape. I am a survivor of slavery and human trafficking. Most of all, I think, I've survived myself.

9to20 Blog, September, 2012

Appendix E

More About the Authors

Becca Johnson

Dr. Johnson has served as trainer, counselor, consulting psychologist, clinical director and aftercare director for numerous anti-trafficking and child abuse organizations. Becca provides support, training and consultation on trauma-sensitive, trauma-focused care.

Dr. Johnson has been a licensed psychologist for 30 years. She also has a passion to "help the hurting heal" and to equip others to help victims on their journey of healing.

Becca consults and provides training for those working with victims of sexual abuse, human trafficking and sexual exploitation. Dr. Johnson has provided trauma recovery workshops at various shelters for victims of sex trafficking in the USA and in over 25 countries.

Becca has served as the Clinical Director for Engedi Refuge, a residential recovery home for women victims of domestic sex trafficking, overseeing individual and group therapy. She has also been actively involved with Agape International Mission (AIM), as former Director of Aftercare Programming and she continues as consulting psychologist for Agape Restoration Center, a residential program for young girls removed from the sex trade in Cambodia.

She also served as International Program and Training Director for Rescue:Freedom International.

Dr. Becca has authored books on helping victims of abuse (*The Journey to Hope – Overcoming Abuse*), on child abuse (*For Their Sake*), trauma recovery (*TRACTS – Trauma Recovery Activities*), guilt (*Good Guilt, Bad Guilt*), and anger (*Overcoming Emotions that Destroy with Chip Ingram*).

Jessa Dillow Crisp

A respected speaker, writer, and mentor, Jessa Dillow Crisp uses her childhood experience of severe abuse and trafficking to illustrate both the stark realities of sex trafficking, and the truth that healing transformation is possible.

After her escape and recovery process, Jessa completed a Master in Clinical Mental Health Counseling as a step towards obtaining a Ph.D. in Clinical Psychology.

In addition to making some of the best lattes in Colorado, Jessa is the co-founder and Executive Director of BridgeHope. Jessa inspires others through speaking engagements around the world, gives hope through mentoring other survivors of human trafficking, and provides high quality training and consultation services to anti-trafficking organizations around the USA.

Karalyn C. Johnson

Karalyn is passionate about people and changing systems to better support individuals and communities. She is completing a Master in Public Policy from the University of Chicago. Prior to her graduate studies, Karalyn taught high school English and History and served on the leadership team for a non-profit organization. Karalyn is an avid reader-writer and has used her talents to add Elisa's engaging story to this book.

Your Response – What You Can Do

What can you do to help? Please consider the following:

1. Donate to survivor-led non-profit organizations. Donated money is primarily used to directly help victims like Elisa.

2. Buy multiple copies of this book to give to others – whether victims, survivors, friends, advocates or helpers (order through Amazon.com).

OR

Sponsor copies to give to victims through LeavingTheLife.org (www.leavingthelife.org). Books will be sent to programs working directly with victims/survivors of sexual exploitation.

3. Let us know what was helpful or hurtful, life-changing or challenging. Email us at Info@leavingthelife.org. Write an honest review of this book on Amazon and Goodreads. Reviews help get books like these into the hands of more people and ultimately, more survivors who need to hear this message of overcoming and hope.

4. Get involved with a local, regional, national or international anti-trafficking organization including groups that are fighting against child abuse, domestic violence, and providing assault-rape crisis services. Time and resources are invaluable in helping survivors begin to heal.

5. Educate others about the global tragedy of child abuse, intimate partner violence, rape, sexual exploitation and human trafficking.

Thank you!